Bakelite

Jewelry

Bakelite

Jewelry

A collector's guide

TONY GRASSO

CHARTWELL
BOOKS, INC.

A QUINTET BOOK

Published by Chartwell Books
A Division of Book Sales, Inc.
114 Northfield Ave
New Jersey 08837

ISBN 0–7858–0276-2

This book was designed and produced by
Quintet Publishing Limited
6 Blundell Street
London N7 9BH

Creative Director: Richard Dewing
Designer: Peter Laws
Project Editor: Anna Briffa
Editor: Sean Connolly
Photographer: Ian Howes

Typeset in Great Britain by
Central Southern Typesetters, Eastbourne
Manufactured in China
by Regent Publishing Services Ltd
Printed in China by Leefung-Asco Printers Ltd

CONTENTS

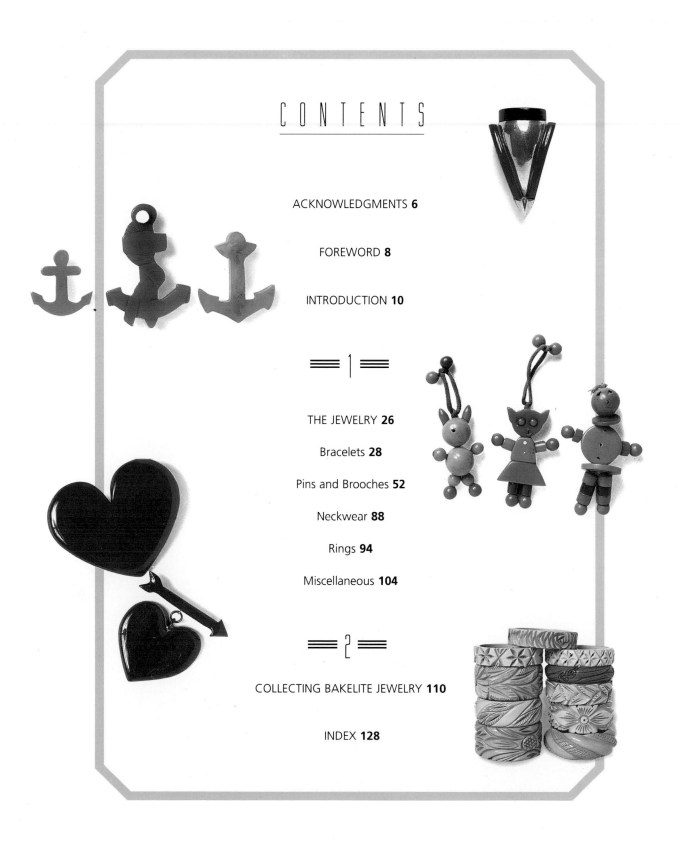

ACKNOWLEDGMENTS

I would like to thank those people responsible for their help in the order in which their influence entered my life. The first to influence me were of course my parents. I thank them, and perhaps someday I will return to architecture, my original profession.

The first influence regarding antiques, however, came from my aunt and uncle, Mary and Fran Hammel. It was from them that I learned about the joy of collecting.

I thank Alice Grasso, former spouse and close friend, who helped me make the transformation from the eclectic to the wonderful world of Bakelite and for our daughter Alex, who grew up on the fields of flea markets and antique shows. She also loves "Bakerlite" as she calls it.

I very much acknowledge Richard Silverman who initiated my interest and my education of plastics in particular. A true Bakelite dealer who always had time to teach people, he lent me his knowledge with the understanding that I share it with others.

To my wife Alexandra, who helps me every weekend after a forty- hour week of her own, I thank her for her love and dedication both to me and to Bakelite; for her patience while writing this book; and for her support in any venture that I choose.

To my daughter Angela, who had to give up some of our time together so I could write, and for the opportunity to enjoy her love of "Bakerbite" as she calls it.

To Abby Nash who renewed my enthusiasm and let me give him some of Richard's knowledge. He just wrote me that his first big show was a Bakelite spectacular! Congratulations.

To Frank Oppel at Book Sales for his referral to Quintet and to Anna Briffa for all her help.

To Dan Nosal for his friendship and for lending me his knowledge of the machinery used to carve Bakelite, and to Ian Howes, a genius with a camera, who "shot" all these pieces, yet gave them life.

To all of my clients who have helped me build my business and have shared with me the joy that Bakelite brings to them.

I also wish to graciously thank Margaret Hamilton who has been a super client and allowed Ian and I to photograph her "to die for" collection and all her "favorite" pieces. Her collection and excitement helped to complete this project.

I also thank Theresa Nosal for lending me her jewelry, and also Alexandra, Alice, Alex, and Angela Grasso for surrendering their favorite pieces of Bakelite for photography.

FOREWORD

fter over a decade of buying and selling Bakelite jewelry, I became frustrated when I bought books that contained other forms of plastic which were mislabeled as Bakelite. So I decided to write a book myself.

The purpose of this book is to tell the story of Bakelite from the ground up and to share my technical knowledge which has grown from experimenting with Bakelite: perhaps also to share some of the joy that I have derived from it. For example, to hear a

teacher describe how my eight-year-old daughter Alex brings bangles to school and teaches her peers to "smell for Bak-er-lite." (She has obviously missed her father's Bostonian pronunciation of "Bak-a-lite"!); or the joy my fifteen-month-old daughter gets from her Bakelite crib toys, and the massive ring of Bakelite balls and tubes which keeps her amused in her playpen at shows; or to see the wide eyes of my wife, when I unwrap a "killer" Bakelite bangle, or a great pin, to fit into the sailing theme that she collects, and which she wears, several pieces at a time; or the amazement on the face of a novice, who just got their first whiff of phenol, or the pride that overcomes them, with their first Bakelite purchase.

This is what a friend, Richard Silverman, told me would happen and at first I doubted, but now I believe him. Because of Richard teaching me all that he knew about Bakelite, and following several years of doing shows set up next to each other, or across an

aisle from each other, I learned that there should not be a competitive nature to Bakelite collecting or selling.

From Richard I learned to bypass the dealer who only had time to sell me, but not teach me. He also showed me that no matter how big you get in the business, you must still have time to educate the newer collector, to inventory lesser-priced stock, to entice a new buyer, and to satisfy the needs of each caliber of collector.

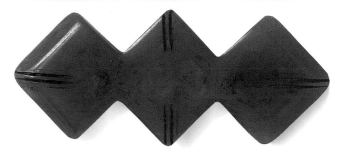

Looking over the slides that were taken for this publication I honestly feel I have accomplished, and kept, a varied selection. I hope that this book will help me keep another promise to Richard, and that is to educate, and help people enter the wonderful world of Bakelite.

I hope that by reading this book you can learn about the technical aspects of collecting Bakelite, and when you are finished I hope you will have a well-balanced background not only of Bakelite itself, but also of the silly nature of collecting this jewelry.

I hope that I can impress upon you that there are a lot of people who would love to enjoy Bakelite but are too bashful to approach someone. These are the people I wrote this book for, and after they read it I would be more than glad to discuss any part of Bakelite with them. If you can, help someone do it.

Although I have a nice collection of home-type accessories – lamps, boxes, dinnerware, and cooking utensils, I sell the jewelry because I have always enjoyed its stylish flair. I wrote this book to show you what's available from top to bottom and to let you decide where to jump in.

INTRODUCTION

Jewelry making, perhaps one of the oldest crafts in recorded history, began as an adornment of natural objects. I feel the first jewelry creation most likely occurred after some prehistoric man found a pretty or rather unusual stone, followed by perhaps a number of feathers, a couple of nuts, and finally a leaf or two (which worked well as accent pieces).

At this point, these treasures were probably inventoried, laid out, then fastened together, in some crude manner. The article soon evolved into a gift of adornment for someone of his liking who, in turn, paraded

BELOW

Celluloid leaf set. All components molded from celluloid (see pages 14–16). Upon close observation you can see mold marks on each piece.

this new acquisition, for the admiration of those in the immediate locale.

The order of things being what it is, we would then find people craving this new form of adornment and wanting pieces of jewelry to complement and finalize their wardrobe.

Soon the jewelry maker would have had a full-time career, gathering trinkets and the like, so that he could mold and fasten them together, creating his most recent work of art. Our hero would barely be able to keep up with the requests of those who wanted to stay abreast of the fashions of the time. In order to keep up with the demand, he would then have had to hire an apprentice. After working well with the master for a while, the apprentice eventually might then have devised his own style and ways of doing things. Before too long, he would have felt that his creations were at least as good as, if not surpassing, those of the master. He would eventually fulfill a commission or two on the side, finding he had a following, before deciding to branch out and establish his own shingle. We can now picture two separate jewelry concerns, in

RIGHT

RIGHT

Belt buckles were popular fashion accessories at the time. 1. They were often made of celluloid. 2. Other examples may have been made of cellulose acetate.

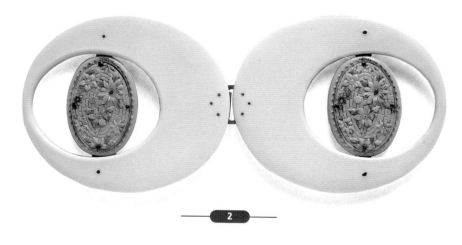

1

2

ABOVE

Celluloid patriotic "Uncle Sam" pin

separate caves, each man exploiting his own fantasies as well as those of the other. This would then mark the birth of jewelry making.

The imaginations of our artisans and their successors would grow in leaps and bounds. Soon, the rocks became gemstones, the fastenings or findings became brass, copper, gold, or silver. The jewelry maker found that the earth is a wonderful supply house.

Ultimately we arrive in the nineteenth century, by which time jewelry had developed a definite purpose. The purpose could be vanity, or perhaps to incite jealousy. The styles and forms of the jewelry varied as much as the number of creators. Some people wore a specific type of jewelry to complement their sense of fashion or to show that they were of comfortable means. Some even wore their jewels to show that they were mourning the death of a loved one. All of these wares, worn for whatever reason, were totally composed of natural substances. Gold, silver, copper, brass, and bronze; diamonds, emeralds, and rubies; amber,

Celluloid lockets. It is very rare to find such items in this condition.

bone, ivory, and Whitby jet — all were natural substances. Some, without saying, were expensive, others were obtained through hours of laborious mining, and still others meant the sacrifice of a particular animal's existence.

In the mid-nineteenth century, however, chemists and scientists began discovering different substances which could be substituted for the expensive or rare type of materials used in jewelry.

Most of the words in our vocabulary have their roots in either the Latin or Greek tongues. "Plastic" is no exception. *Plassein*, the word meaning "to mold," was taken from the Greeks. It has been used through the years to blanket an entire field of materials.

Even natural proteins such as tortoiseshell, amber, horn, and shellacs, have been lumped into this category of plastics. Therefore, I will do my best to distinguish between natural, semisynthetic, and synthetic plastics.

GUTTA PERCHA

For hundreds of years, jewelry makers had been using natural plastics, such as amber, horn, and tortoiseshell to finish their creations. Gutta percha, a combination of proteins from the Malaysian rubber tree, with various fillers, was introduced by an Englishman years before. By the

Two celluloid pins. 1. The army soldier was marketed under "My Buddy." 2. The bellboy is quite rare and popular among collectors.

nineteenth century it was being used for hundreds of purposes, one of which was jewelry making. This material, which is extremely hard but rubbery, was molded or carved to the desired effect. Since gutta percha is mostly black in color, it was used extensively in jewelry worn by mourners. Picture frames and other household accessories were also made in black, brown, and, rarely, a grayish brown. Unfortunately, gutta percha dried up over years of exposure to the elements, so we find pieces today with heavy cracks, chips, and even some broken in multiple pieces.

It has become extremely difficult to find a piece that has not been repaired in some fashion. Also, if you do find what you think is a perfect piece, look it over carefully. The chances are you are holding another substance, which an unknowledgable dealer would call gutta percha.

I have seen a variety of materials marked gutta percha. Celluloid, bog oak, and even amber, have been mistaken for the rubbery substance.

Keep an eye out: you may make the find of the year, through a case of mistaken identity.

CELLULOID

While the nineteenth century progressed, so too did the developments of semisynthetic plastics. Throughout the century, several prominent chemists, scientists, and inventors piggybacked upon one another's developments and discoveries.

In 1842, a Swiss chemist by the name of Schoenbine developed a substance by joining sulfuric and nitric acids. When he added sawdust and cotton fibers he found that he had a fantastic material for explosives. The product was referred to as cellulose nitrate. For several years, Schoenbine enjoyed exclusivity for his product.

An English inventor by the name of Alexander Parkes was also working with cellulose nitrate. In 1853, he found that by introducing different chemicals such as camphor, he could work cellulose nitrate into a flowing substance, which could be molded into finished products. Once the thinners dissipated from the formula, he had a solid, hard mass, which retained whatever shape or mold into which it had been poured. Parkes marketed his discovery under the name of Parkesine. He set out to manufacture it with a business associate, but due to underfunding and legal battles they ultimately failed. To make matters worse, in 1884, Parkes even lost all patent rights to a fellow inventor, the American John Hyatt. Hyatt and his brother Isaiah were experimenting with cellulose

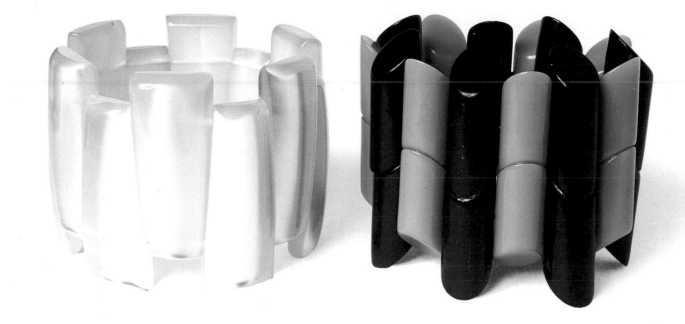

Two celluloid bracelets. The white one has been opalized through the use of ground shell.

nitrate. They worked on improving the formula and, upon finding a satisfactory material to replace ivory, drew a patent for their new product. They called their invention celluloid, for which they set up a company, known as The American Celluloid Company.

Celluloid was soon adopted around the world as a miracle of science. It was soon manufactured in North America, Europe, and Asia. Household items, such as handles for silverware, picture frames, and dresser sets, were springing up in every home. The fashion industry idolized celluloid. Manufacturers of hair combs, hat ornaments, buckles, buttons, and other jewelry utilized this plastic. Now the less well off could relish those things which until now had been fashioned from ivory and tortoiseshell. They no longer had to expend large sums of their savings to compete with the more fortunate. Celluloid was used for almost everything. The Hyatt brothers improved and perfected the processing aspect, as well as developing better casting and molding techniques, which are still in use today.

The Hyatts developed and patented the injection and compression molding techniques, which were the most commonly used. Extrusion, a sheeting as well as tubing method, was soon seen as an exceptional method by which to produce bracelets and bangles. It was followed by blow molding, which was the method of molding used to produce hollow items. Molding allowed for the production of pins, earrings, and neckwear, all resembling tortoiseshell, amber, and even ivory. The Europeans progressed in celluloid production, and the French revolutionized the transition from ivory to the much more affordable, and accessible, celluloid.

Soon people all over the world were stockpiling large caches of "French ivory." The French developed a celluloid with lines, meant to resemble the cross-hatching nature of the African elephant tusk.

Several years ago, I actually had occasion to witness the effect this has had on some people. While at a yard sale in Massachusetts, I saw an extensive dresser set on a table. The set, which consisted of combs, brushes, mirror, containers, and more, was marked $200. Although I was interested, I felt that the price was much too high, so I asked if perhaps the owner "could do better." I was informed that the set was made of ivory, and had been retrieved by her grandfather, as a wedding gift for his bride when he left Europe during the war. Upon closer inspection, I noticed that each piece had been hot-stamped with the words "French ivory." Being of the opinion that it is often a futile effort to educate someone about their belongings, I convinced myself that I really didn't have to own one of the nicest celluloid dresser sets I had ever laid eyes on.

Urea-formaldehyde fish.

GALALITH

During the last decades of the nineteenth century, technicians through-out Europe were dabbling with different plant and animal proteins, to bring forth the new "miracle plastic." Just before the turn of the century, a German chemical engineer, Adolph Spitteler, was experimenting with different chemicals in order to find a viable substitute for horn. During the course of his work he found that if he blended formaldehyde with a protein called casein, which he derived from spoiled milk, the process yielded an extremely hard material. In 1897, he patented his discovery, and the substance was dubbed galalith.

This protein plastic, although a splash in the pan, became a widely used base, for articles such as buttons, dress clips, hat ornaments, buckles, and also jewelry. This was because galalith lent itself easily to carving and, when polished, took on a long-lasting luster. Casein plastics were used throughout Europe, again as a replacement for tortoiseshell, horn, and ivory. Pen manufacturers found the new plastic to be excellent for fountain-pen cases. Millions of knitting needles were formed.

ABOVE

An assortment of animals. Some are galalith, while others are Bakelite. The galalith ones are a bright white, have a very crackled texture and are badly warped.

Galalith, because it would accept such a high polish, easily made its way into the fashion industry. Much harder than celluloid, it drifted into the commercial and industrial sector, but, because of certain limitations (larger pieces warped or splintered), proved to be used primarily in the button industry.

Until now, all of the semisynthetic plastics would be characterized as thermoplastics. In lay terms, this means that, with the molding processes developed by the Hyatts, they could be heated and molded into nearly any shape. Manufacturers had artisans carve molds for flowers and leaves, which were filled with the heated mixture. Different polymers were used for particular objects, depending on their pigmentation qualities. Others were utilized because of their hardness and durability.

Each polymer could be reheated and reformed, even though it had been cured. The molecular structure of each thermoplastic is the same; the molecules are grouped together, by an electromagnetic charge. The charge that bundles the fibers of thermoplastics is weak and cannot withstand heat, and much like a handful of pickup sticks, they will slide by one another under reheating, thus explaining the flowing nature of hot plastics.

DR. LEO HENDRICK BAEKELAND

In 1863, Parkes was trying to get his Parkesine produced. The Hyatts were working on a substitute for ivory. And in Ghent, Belgium, Rosalia Baekeland gave birth to a boy, Leo. Neither she nor her husband Karel had any idea of the gift they had given the world.

Baekeland attended the Technical School of Ghent, until graduation in 1880. He matriculated to the University of Ghent, graduating with a Bachelor of Science degree in 1882. Continuing his education by 1884, he graduated *maxima cum laude* with a doctorate in natural science. He stayed at the University several more years, as a professor of chemistry and physics, also winning prizes, competitions, and honors for his work in related fields.

Dr. Baekeland emigrated to the United States in 1889. As a means of support, he took employment with a photographic firm. While with this firm, he continued experimenting in his own laboratory at home, where he eventually formulated a light-sensitive photographic paper, which he patented under the name Velox. From 1893 to 1899, Baekeland headed his own firm, the Neperd Chemical Company, which produced primarily Velox, but also other papers and chemicals for the photographic trade. In 1899, he sold both his company and the patent rights for Velox paper to the Eastman-Kodak Company for approximately $1,000,000.

Unemployed, but extremely well off, Baekeland continued his research. He managed to develop yet another product, an electrolytic cell, for Hooker Electrochemical Company, in upstate New York. By this time, Baekeland had set up residence in Yonkers, New York, where he had set up a laboratory, so he could further his research on shellacs.

The condensation of products, emanating from the union of carbolic acid (phenol) and formaldehyde, had been researched, by Adolf von Baeyer in the 1870's. Unfortunately, von Baeyer abandoned his work, because the long and tedious process yielded an inferior and brittle product, which had no purpose.

Dr. Baekeland used the basic thoughts behind von Baeyer's studies, added various bases, and a soluble solution to perfect not only the first phenolic resin, but also the first thermosetting plastic. Production started in his garage, in Yonkers, in 1907. He moved operations to Perth Amboy, New Jersey, in 1909, and by 1930 he was emitting thousands of pounds of resin, from a 128-acre plant at Bound Brook, New Jersey, as well as from plants in both England and Germany.

ABOVE

Dr. Baekeland was an inventor of great magnitude, with a keen interest in chemical and electrical research and development.

Cast phenolic tubes. They were probably destined to become buckles, pins, etc. after slicing and tumbling.

THERMOSETTING PLASTICS

Up until the discovery of phenol-formaldehyde, as mentioned earlier, all semisynthetic plastics were of a thermo nature. The materials in question were molded, through the use of solvents and a heat process, into whatever end-product was desired. Immediately, or years later, the same product when exposed to heat would melt down again, and could be "recycled" for other purposes. Baekeland had discovered a component which, through extreme heat and pressure, could be cast or molded into a product which could never be remelted. This is classified as a thermosetting plastic. The molecular structure of Bakelite is different from that of other plastics. As mentioned previously thermoplastics are like pickup sticks, or bristles on a broom. They are held together by a weak electromagnetic charge. When these molecules are heated, they simply move by each other, and the bond is broken. The result of heating a thermoplastic is a limp pool of molecules which, if left to cool, will result in a puddle-like form; but these molecules can be reheated and reshaped into another form, while still flowing.

With the phenolics, the molecular structure is more like that of a mass of tangled hair removed from a hairbrush. The chemical bond,

Children's fork and spoon with Bakelite handles and mold-injected Scotties. The dogs would have originally been white, but the color has altered due to oxidation.

referred to as cross-linking, is a much stronger bond than the weaker, electromagnetic bond. This structure can endure extremely high temperatures, as well as hundreds of thousands of volts of electricity. Phenol objects, because of their structure, also resist chemicals to a much greater extent.

This can be exemplified by a predicament I found myself in a few years ago. While shopping at a flea market, I bought a thick, wide, and beautifully carved Bakelite bangle, at an extremely low price. The only problem with my find was that the bangle evidently had met up with that same mad painter that so many collectibles stray across. After examining the piece for a day or two, I tried to cut this new modification, with several solvents, with little success. Merely dulling, and somewhat fading, the coating, I decided the bangle was worthless the way it was, so I dropped it into a coffee can filled with nail polish remover, covered it up, and stuck it under a bench, so the children wouldn't get into it. I totally forgot about the bracelet, until a few months later. I decided to drop a few more bangles into the same can when, much to my surprise, they would not all fit. I pulled out the bracelets to find that on the bottom was the very same bracelet I had soaked some months before. The piece which had bathed in nail polish remover was now totally clean, but extremely dull. The dull finish, which was remedied by a good polishing,

Bakelite cigarette holder with
original case.

netted a beautiful piece of artistry, showing no sign whatsoever that it
had spent years wearing this coat of paint. I have since kept track of the
pieces that go into the coffee can. I have soaked quite a few painted
pieces of jewelry in this can, but the only ones that make it through the
process have been phenolics. I have soaked some that were made of
molded celluloid, and acrylics. I can only assume they are still in the
acetone solution because, as hard as I have looked, I just can't seem to
find them. I did retrieve a cellulose acetate piece, which did not totally
dissolve. Unfortunately, it merely crumbled away at my first attempt to
polish it. I totally discourage this kind of experimenting, as nail polish
remover is very flammable and, if you are a novice to the plastics, you
may destroy some very valuable pieces of jewelry.

Phenolics not only withstand this exposure, but show little or no sign
that they were ever exposed in the first place. Before the development of
Bakelite, all thermoplastics had been composed with, or based on, a
number of animal or vegetable proteins. Bakelite was the first totally
manmade element plastic. Because of its specific resistance to melting,
Bakelite immediately became the main staple of the electronics industry.
Bakelite will never melt, or ignite, no matter how much heat or voltage is
applied. It will, however, take on a burgundy-colored burn mark, from an
open flame or extreme heat. We will explore this further on.

Bakelite napkin rings, one with wheels. These have remained immensely popular to this day, particularly in Europe.

BAKELITE

Baekeland did not just walk into his lab one afternoon and come out with the solution to the world's needs. He did spend several years working on different formulas and ingredients; however, the final outcome of his recipe was, indeed, stumbled upon.

While working toward a different type of plastic, one that could be substituted for shellac, he mixed carbolic acid and formaldehyde, but was looking for a totally different result. He only realized what he had developed when he tried to reheat his formula. He found that, no matter how much he heated the mass of chemicals, it would not change form. He found the new concoction not only different from those produced by his fellow chemists, but a new material that should be patented immediately. He patented his discovery in 1907. Baekeland soon learned that his formula could either be cast or molded.

By way of explanation, molding, the more common means of finishing plastics, is a process by which molten polymers are poured into various molds, creating shells for such things as telephones, radio cabinets, and the like. Casting, the medium by which most Bakelite jewelry derived, was the process which used extreme heat and pressure to thrust forth a cylinder, tube, rod, or sheet, much as a frosting or cookie machine will shoot out a tube in the shape of, for example, a dog. The tube will then be sliced into several dog-shaped cookies. This is somewhat simplified, but gives an idea of what was happening to the phenolic resins at the manufacturing level.

The world embraced Baekeland's wonder child immediately. The quickest acquisitions were by electrical companies. Soon the Bakelite company was selling resin, castings, and moldings to companies everywhere. When Bakelite was discovered, Baekeland was working with an amber-colored resin. He quickly found that fillers could be added, not only to enhance the color, but also to strengthen the object.

He experimented with wood flour, cotton fiber, asbestos, and even metals to strengthen the emulsion. With the strength aspect now behind him, he eventually worked out a satisfactory pigmentation process.

ABOVE

Bakelite key ring with Scottie dog

"THE MATERIAL OF A THOUSAND USES"

Bakelite was soon promoted, by Baekeland and his public relations people, as "the material of a thousand uses." As a promotion point, Baekeland compiled a list of about forty industries that could implement his resin. By the late thirties it was said that it would be harder to formulate a list of forty industries that did *not* use Bakelite. The latter years of the second decade of the twentieth century found Bakelite being used primarily as an insulator. Objects such as plugs, electrical boxes, handles for electrical units, and telephones were the first offspring of Baekeland's resin. Most of these were in either brown, black, and occasionally, clear amber. In the twenties, by experimenting with pigmentation, Bakelite took on a "whole new color." The Bakelite Corporation sent out an army of salespeople, armed with salesman's sample kits, containing an array of colors, swirls, and pearlescent disks. Manufacturers could now cast things in living color. Kitchens took on hues of red, green, orange, and white (soon to be an opaque mustard color, which will be discussed later). Pot handles, spatulas, eggbeaters, bowls, dishes, cups, and saucers all took on the Bakelite colors.

It was the mid-twenties that casters and molders started tempting the American public with Bakelite jewelry. The "Roaring Twenties" found the American woman enveloped in Bakelite jewelry. With multicolored beads and bangles, the "flappers" of the day went off to the "speak-easy" of their choice, to dazzle their friends. Electronics concerns also relished in these new colors, because they were no longer restricted to the wood, drab browns, and blacks, to which they had become accustomed. They could now produce their wares in dazzling colors. Any family could sport a new radio in burgundy and yellow, or a new phonograph or television in shades of red and black, with amber knobs.

By the thirties, the Bakelite company was in full swing, and a serious number of casters and molders were now producing tons of Bakelite daily. A newcomer, The Catalin Corporation (started in 1929), developed a new translucent pigmentation process, which was added to the old phenolic resin compound. The new company embarked on its own aggressive advertising campaign. Obviously, all the hype and marketing succeeded and, by 1933, Bakelite had become ubiquitous.

Picture this typical thirties routine. A couple shut off their Bakelite-clad alarm clock and turn on the Catalin radio. Then they flip the Bakelite bathroom light switch, lift the Bakelite toilet-seat cover, shower with soap retrieved from the Bakelite soap holder, give their teeth a quick brushing with their Bakelite toothbrush, lather up with a Bakelite soap brush, and shave with a Bakelite-handled shaver. Back in their bedroom to dress, they button the Bakelite buttons on their shirt, blouse, pants, or skirt. Perhaps he would insert a pair of Bakelite cuff links into his shirt cuffs, while she put on her belt with the Bakelite buckle. After blow-drying her hair with the Bakelite-cased hair drier, she brushes it out with the

RIGHT AND OPPOSITE

Once manufacturers moved away from browns and black and toward developing, colors the fun possibilities became exciting and endless.

Stanley Products hairbrush. A nice finishing touch is the pretty set of red Bakelite bow barrettes, to keep her from worrying about a bad hair day.

Our phenol duo now goes to the kitchen and, as a joint venture, prepares breakfast. She whips up a few hotcakes on the griddle with the Bakelite handle. Using the Bakelite-handled spatula to flip them, she reaches for the cute Bakelite mushroom salt and peppers kept on the back of the stove. Her husband, having laid out the polka-dot-handled flatware, is carefully arranging napkins into several Bakelite napkin rings. They hastily toss the Bakelite dishware into the sink, the husband goes to the garage, starts the car, grabs the Bakelite steering wheel, and, with the use of the Bakelite gearshift knob, drops the car into reverse and waits for his wife, who has returned to the bedroom to put on the new "Philadelphia Set" that her friends have been waiting to see.

The scenario I have painted may have been tainted by just a small bit of envy, but it does point out the role that Bakelite played in everyday life in the thirties. The cast phenolic resin tubes, rods, and sheets, by now had been processed into functional household items. Just as important was the role Bakelite played in providing beauty or simply whimsical diversion from the economic gloom of that decade. That led to the development of the fantasy world of Bakelite jewelry.

ABOVE

Not only could colors be used endlessly, but it almost became a challenge to find a use that Bakelite itself could not be put to.

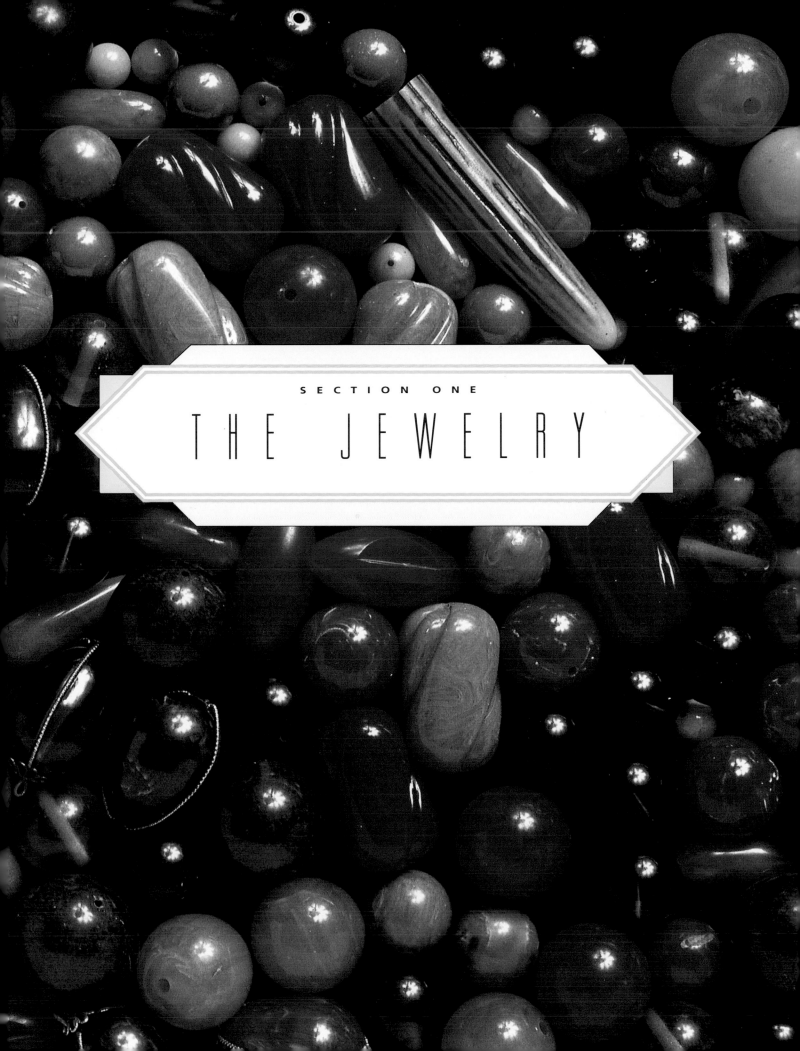

SECTION ONE

THE JEWELRY

BRACELETS

B racelets are probably the most diversified member of the Bakelite family. Coming in all shapes and sizes, they are now more plentiful than pins, earrings, and all the other pieces combined. It has been said that 40 percent of all the cast phenolic produced, by weight, was manufactured into buttons. It seems that over the years many of these buttons were discarded, along with the garments they were attached to. The bracelet seems to account for approximately 60 percent of the Bakelite pieces I see today. These were probably the first pieces produced, because of the ease in which they were manufactured. The simple bangle came on the scene during the twenties and by the mid-thirties was transformed into the wide, thick and "carved to death" pieces that are so sought after today.

As time progressed, so did the design of Bakelite bracelets. Companies that had previously restricted their business to carving wood products soon retooled and expanded into the Bakelite market. The designs were simple to start with, but soon the better carvers were given more complex designs to reproduce in Bakelite form. After the bangle was appropriated from the tube, it was put onto a jigging machine, which consisted of an indexing head, in order to calibrate the carving into windows or scenic sections. The actual carving was done with a range of tools. Sometimes the piece was put on a lathe and turned to the desired pattern. Often a rotary-type tool with various styled bits was used in conjunction with a tracery mechanism or guide to cut the less complicated patterns (for instance, a leaf and flower). The more complicated heavy relief pieces were pattern-scribed first, then were extended freehandedly with a rotary-type tool. This could be used to carve and get under the backs of, say, a rose, so that the petals have the relief, or 3-D effect, found on some of the "big" or "heavy" carved items. This rotary tool was also utilized freehand, to carve most of the "reverse-carved" pieces. After the carving was finished for the day, most

1

2

3

of the work was tumbled in huge drums filled with fillers and various grit silica. Each batch went through a rough, medium, and fine process, before a final detergent and polishing stage. Some of the "heavy" carved pieces were polished with a cloth or felt wheel using a pumice solution, to diminish any "wheel," or carving marks before engaging in the cleaning and polishing stages. A few select pieces had the extreme edges finely polished, after dancing with a medium grit solution in the tumbler. This would leave the edges with a glass-like finish, with the inner depths of the carving in a matte-like or frosted finish. This is an extremely beautiful effect, especially on some of the clear pieces.

BANGLES

Bangles led the way onto the fashion scene in the mid-twenties. Take a phenolic tube, slice off a couple of pieces, and you have a group of bangles. The fashionable woman of the postwar twenties was now looking toward costume jewelry to complement her attire. She could no longer afford the real thing, and she was heading into the "Great Depression." For the time being, she would have to adjust, to imitation jet, amber, ivory, and tortoiseshell.

During the "Roaring Twenties," the idea of eight to ten thin, multicolored bangles over each wrist finished off the costume of the day. They also produced a relaxing clunking sound when walking or shaking around on the dance floor.

Novelty companies would buy the cast tubes, slice thousands of bracelets from them, polish the edges, and sell them to the five-and-dimes, or even sell to some of the costume houses, such as Coro or Trifari. These bangles were sliced at quarter, half, three-quarter, and full inch thickness; some had the edges rounded, some were left squared, and the retail prices ranged from 5¢ to 75¢ each. I have picked up several sets which were never worn and still had the foil labels attached. The most expensive I have found was a set of three plain bangles, two at a quarter inch, and one at three-quarters of an inch. The three were bound with a Coro label, which called for a $2 price for all three.

2

3

ABOVE AND LEFT

Examples of bangles that were
turned on the lathe. 1., 2. Some
were produced in just one color,
while others were dyed after
carving. 3. This magnificent green
bangle still has the plastic-coated
string intact.

RIGHT

Faceting became a very popular
technique, both on clear and
opaque bangles. These stacks here
show the variety of sizes and colors
produced. It became fashionable to
wear up to seven or eight bangles
on one arm.

1

"End of Day," several colors in one. Very desirable.

From the plain uncarved bangle, jewelry makers developed basic pieces that had been turned and carved on a lathe, to give the piece a bit of dimension. A couple of lines soon grew into pieces that were of different planes. The bangle soon progressed into the single-dimension flower and leaf stage, which could be jigged, without a lot of time or labor. This design is plentiful, and I think much of it drags over from the Nouveau era. There has also been a large number of different simple carvings done. Many of the bangles were done in a faceted pattern, varying in both pattern style and thickness. You can often find bangles with the same size faceting, and this makes a very pretty collection,

when wearing several multicolored bracelets with a translucent, or opaque, pigmentation.

As the skills of the carvers grew keener, the bangles wore coats of finely, or dramatically, carved scenes. It is not uncommon to find a beautifully carved panorama, seascape of a beach scene, with a few palm trees, the setting sun, and a bird or two searching the waves for dinner. There are bracelets that are totally carved in the texture of pineapples.

Fantastic stacks of thick heavy-carved bangles. 1., 2. Flowers and leaves seem to be predominant designs, often extremely intricate. 3. An impressive tower of white and butterscotch heavy-carved bangles. The white ones have darkened through oxidation.

You will find heavily carved tropical vegetation, large flowers with leaves, and stems, all in very deep relief.

Other designs worth mentioning corresponded to the Deco or Machine Age. These were actually done in patterns resembling gears and sprockets. These geometrics of the Deco era took their place in Bakelite jewelry as they had in the other areas of the decorative arts.

GEOMETRICS

The geometric style of the Deco era was adapted to Bakelite jewelry in several different ways. Some of the better-known and adventurous designers of this era took on the task of associating their names with that of Bakelite. One of the foremost was a New York designer, Belle Kogan who took the polka dot and stretched it into an oval, and progressively elongated this figure. Some of the bracelets contained a series of one-inch ovals, others may have had two-inch ovals right up to the point where two ovals were used to circumference a single bangle.

ABOVE, LEFT AND RIGHT

Examples of geometric designs from the Deco era. 1. A pair of carved and cut-through bangles. 2. A pair of white bangles showing varied oxidation. 3. A magnificent group of Belle Kogan bracelets.

The bracelets, all in a two-tone motif, were done by taking a blank from a phenolic tube, carving out the appropriate oval, and mold-injecting a different color phenolic into the void. The end-product was then ground flush, the edges were eased, and the piece went to the tumblers for sanding and polishing. These pieces are somewhat rare and are still a very desirable find today.

During the early fifties this mold-injection process was carried a bit further, and the result was the gumdrop (multicolored and varied-size dots) bracelet and the much sought-after bow-tie bracelet.

The "Philadelphia" style has become a much treasured geometric. This style earned the name at an antiques show in Philadelphia. A dealer who was offering a piece for sale was amazed when a bidding war erupted between two people wanting this megapiece. It went to the highest bidder, and has been known as the "Philadelphia Bracelet" ever since.

Consisting of five triangular or sometimes disk-shaped pieces, bonded together, then adhered to the adapted top of a hinged bracelet, the "Philadelphia Bracelet" represents the purity of Bakelite's role in Deco or Machine Age design.

ABOVE

Examples of bangles with stripes;
1. hinged and bangle stripes; 2. thin
two-tone bangles.

STRIPES

Another sibling to the geometric approach is the stripe bracelet. I have
had stripes in two different forms, the more common being the solid
laminate. This was commonly done by laminating three or more pieces of
tube stock, to form a multicolored pattern and to suit the fancy of the
designer. Most times uncarved, there was the "can't leave it alone"
breed, who just had to facet it, or put it on a lathe, and score it a bit, or
even create the "Saturn" style bracelet which resembles pictures of the
planet with the many rings which surround it.

The other type of stripe I have uncovered is the molded type. If I had
not dropped a stripe bracelet a couple of years ago, I probably would
have agreed that all the jewelry was cast. This piece broke apart,
revealing that it comprised three molded pieces, which had been glued
together. This is the only piece I have ever come across, so possibly it was
a prototype, or perhaps from a home jewelry kit.

Striped bangles and bracelets were made using a multitude of designs and techniques, as illustrated by the pieces on this page. They ranged from; 1. the very simple stripe to, 2. two-tone stripes. 3. Sometimes they would be cast half and half. 4. Other times they would be in combination with carving or, 5. faceting.

1

2

3

5

4

Possibly one of the most fun and whimsical designs of the era – the polka dot – circles of one color on a contrasting background.

POLKA DOTS

Polka dots are the bracelets that I enjoy the most. They were made primarily by drilling holes in a somewhat thick blank. The holes were drilled using an indexing head and a counter-bore. Then rods were driven into the holes, cut off, ground down, and tumbled, and polished. Generally, these funky pieces were done in extremely contrasting color schemes. Black with white (now mustard), black with pink (now orange), mostly with dark tubes and light dots, or vice versa.

Unfortunately the polka dot has caught the brunt of the "new Bakelite" scare. At some of the Manhattan shows, it has become a rarity even to sell one of these optical pleasures, because some of the dealers have scared the consumers by telling them "that's new" or "that's made up." I recall an instance in 1994 when a young lady stopped in at a Manhattan show and showed me two beautiful polka-dot bracelets she had just purchased at the 26th Street Flea Market. These two polka dots represented her first Bakelite purchase and they were her membership card, into the Bakelite collectors' club. She had spent $350 on the pair, and showed them proudly to a dealer on the floor, only to have him rain all over her parade. He told her that "those things are new Bakelite." I

knew who the particular dealer was, and although he has an extensive inventory of super Bakelite pieces, his background knowledge of the product is very limited, so I mentioned to her that he tells everyone who approaches him that their purchases (if they were not bought from him) are new, and I explained to her that the green bracelet, in fact, had white dots, not the mustard color she perceived, and that this bracelet had never even been polished in a decade or so. I also mentioned that the same dealer had an identical black with red dot bracelet in his case, so why was hers new and his old? I sent her to a dealer who has achieved an extensive knowledge and has been selling Bakelite for almost twenty

years. This dealer told her the same thing I had, almost verbatim, so this newly ordained collector was able to leave the show with renewed confidence.

I have seen this same dealer and others act out his "Bakelite Police" routine repeatedly over the last few years. I don't understand why this is done, perhaps because the great pieces are getting scarce, and the dealer figures the customer will sell it cheaply; or perhaps it is a jealousy thing, that he was not the seller. The end-result of this man's ignorance was nearly to cast out another new enthusiast from the Bakelite collectors' family. I have been shown quite a few polka-dot pieces, and I have seen a few done in acrylic or styrene. Yet to see even a Shultz piece (see page 120) that was sold to anybody as an original is an extreme scarcity. Some dealers accuse some polka dots of being a fifties piece, of Marblette origin, yet they command an extremely high price for mold-injected gumdrops or bow-ties, which were also done in the fifties. My recommendation is that you consult a couple of dealers for an opinion or if you find a polka dot that you love and can afford, just go for it, because the work is there. I think the dots are definitely the funkiest of the bracelets, and look better stacked up on one's wrist than any other designs of bracelets.

HINGED BRACELETS

Hinged bracelets seemed to come alive as the dealers found the "to die for" carvings that the collector was seeking. In my earlier stages of selling Bakelite I found the hinged bracelet was somewhat limited to the woman, or sometimes man, who could not fit a bangle over their hand. The main focus during the eighties seemed to turn toward the bangle, perhaps because the buyers were stacking them wrist to elbow and talking about "that clunky noise" which came from the banging of several bangles. In recent years, I have noticed a lot of collectors wearing the sole hinged bracelet for a somewhat formal look.

If you are not aware of this style, the hinged bracelet is the by-

BELOW

A group of heavy-carved hinged bracelets.

product of cutting a tube in half, and ultimately joining the two pieces, with a spring-loaded hinge which was fastened to the Bakelite with screws or pins. The opposite side of the hinged portion opens, and this type of bracelet can easily be slid across the wrist, thereby alleviating a need for a large opening.

When cutting a tube for making a hinged bracelet, the tube used is either oval-shaped, or there are two cuts made in a circular piece. Most of the hinged bracelets have had some of the circumference removed, and the result is an oval-shaped piece which fits snugly to the wrist and lacks the motion that bangles have.

The two pieces that make up a hinged piece were first carved. Some were carved only on the top section, while others had the bottoms shaped or carved according to the fancy of the worker. After carving (I hope by now you know the next step), of course, they went to the tumblers and polishers. Then they would have the hinge affixed and they were wrapped and packaged for distribution.

The famed "Philadelphia Bracelet" was of this species. I have had several exquisitely carved hinged bracelets, some of which I have kept .

BELOW

Spectacular group of hinged geometric and laminated bracelets, possibly of European origin.

Many of the techniques seen previously were also applied to hinged bracelets. 1. Examples from (left to right) Germany, France, and the United States. 2. An exquisite clear, unpigmented secretaries' hinged bracelet. Very valuable. 3. When this clear eggplant hinged bracelet is held up to the sunlight, it will produce blue, red, purple, and amber light. 4. An example of simple, but elegant vine work.

Generally, "stretchy" or elastic
bracelets tend to be of fairly simple
designs, using plain pieces of
Bakelite.

ELASTIC BRACELETS

The elastic or "stretchy" bracelet is exactly what it sounds like, a
conglomeration of Bakelite pieces that were drilled and held together by
an elasticized string which was drawn through the holes and knotted. I
really have no clue as to why it developed, other than to fit a large-
handed wearer. For the most part stretchies are simple — some with
faceting, some with no carving whatsoever. I have had stretchies that
consisted solely of a number of pieces of rod stock cut to length, drilled,
and strung. Occasionally I get a piece that looks to have been a bangle
that was cut up and strung together. These are the only pieces I have
found that were intricately carved. I really can't be sure whether these
were in fact bangles in the beginning, but upon inspection the drilled
holes showed there was no color variation. The mah-jongg and domino
bracelets I make take over a year for the drilled holes to return to the
same color as the outer portion. These bracelets certainly come in handy
when a woman is complaining about the small sizes of the other
bracelets. I have made several want-to-be collectors glow by slipping a
stretchy over my own large hand, and then offering it for them to try.

1. Sometimes, and usually originating in Europe, they have metal findings. 2., 3. Oftentimes, the pieces are of two or three different shapes or sizes. 4. Carving and faceting are rare, but examples do crop up occasionally, like these reverse-carved medallion bracelets.

LEFT AND BELOW

A pile of mah-jongg jewelry bracelets, and a pile of domino bracelets. The mah-jongg and domino jewelry are considered by the "Bakelite Police" as "new" bakelite. Anyone knowledgeable can see they are old gaming pieces.

CUFFS

I don't have a lot to say about this category of bracelet. Most cuffs (save about 10 percent) that I have found seem to be the product of the Marblette Company, which would put them into the early forties to early fifties vintage. I have found that most are very plain, in terms of carving, and also most are of an oval composition. I have found that most seem to be uncomfortable for today's women and have sold very few over the years, only to the occasional woman who can't fit the bangle over her hand. They have a tendency to fall off of a slender wrist, so your wrist has to be full enough to keep the cuff stationary, but small enough to get the narrow space over the wrist.

CHILDREN'S OR MAIDEN BRACELETS?

Under this category of bracelet I feel I may be a bit out on a limb. During my second or third year of selling Bakelite, I stumbled upon a very small round object made of Bakelite. The dealer who had it informed me that he thought it was perhaps a large napkin ring. We were both a bit uncomfortable with this idea, but it was very inexpensive (I think a dollar

BELOW

A group of "children's" bracelets with an adult's to show scale. Hard to price because children don't get a Bakelite allowance!

LEFT

Two lanes of bracelets; children's with adults'.

or two) so I took it. After examining this piece a little further I decided it was a bit large for a napkin ring, so I gave it to my daughter to wear as a bracelet. Over the next few months I came across a few more of these mystery pieces — all plain, in various widths, between three-quarters of an inch and an inch and a half, each with the same inside diameter. I eventually came across a similar piece that was heavily carved, so I became convinced that these were in fact children's bracelets.

After several years of picking up at least 50 or so various pieces with which I could surprise my children, I had a woman approach my booth at a show and inquire if I had any Bakelite maiden bracelets. I was initially confused, but, after the nice explanation she gave me, decided I liked her

Bakelite watch (it works!).

terminology. After researching the word "maiden" with Mr. Webster — his reference was "an unmarried woman, a virgin, a Scottish beheading device, a horse that has never won a race" — I have since reverted back to calling these smaller baubles children's bracelets. I am extremely grateful to her for her enlightenment because I do recall finding a piece or two with an intermediate circumference which may indeed be what she was referring to, or possibly just a round piece of Bakelite that was salvaged from a discarded item. I find it comforting to learn new things about Bakelite, so I will leave the descriptive terminology up to you, the beholder.

FANTASY BRACELETS

In my mind, "fantasy bracelets" encompass all of the crazy, wacky, fun pieces that cannot be listed under the previously mentioned headings. These include mostly fruits and vegetables, and other dangly items. Most of these had Bakelite pieces that were hung, from metal or celluloid chain, and some are very desirable from the collector's standpoint. There were also charm bracelets made with Bakelite pieces. One of the nice pieces I have seen recently had a sailing motif, with the sailboat, anchor, ship's wheel, etc. Unfortunately, these fantasy pieces are very rare today, mostly because they were of a more delicate nature and could not withstand the test of time, so they are generally very expensive, when you can find them.

I will move onto another favorite topic, which is that silly old Bakelite pin. Too much fun to be referred to as a brooch, the pin is that awkward, frivolous little sister of the Bakelite clan, that took the thirties by storm, passed on, but was reincarnated in this decade, much to the delight of today's collector.

Charm-type bracelets, some with fruits.

Charm bracelet with an oriental theme. Some pieces are on a Bakelite backing.

PINS AND BROOCHES

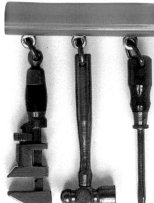

Pins are the devil-may-care members of Bakelite jewelry. In hindsight, one may notice that the pin fulfilled all of the frustrated dreams and fantasies that the bracelet was unable to grasp. Mostly composed of cast sheets, the blanks used for carving Bakelite pins vary both in size and thickness. A select few I have found were actually cut from, and parallel to, the sides of large (6-inch diameter) tubes. There are a lot of pieces that were sliced from the end of a smaller (2–3-inch diameter) tube in the same manner as bangles. Some of these were eased at the square surfaces and left as is, while others spent an allotted period of time with the carver.

The original pins were totally plain white (now mustard), black, or brown. It can be seen that some of these were wrought from the sides of tube stock, as they display the telltale hollow on the underside. As the engineers and chemists advanced the color range, soon the pin was given a wardrobe of glamorous color. They added layers of these colors as soon as the laminating process was perfected. The pin rapidly expanded into

ABOVE AND BELOW

Just about anything imaginable was used as the basis for a pin design. 1. This pin, possibly of German origin, has actual working tools attached to the Bakelite handle. 2. The Scottie dog became one of the most popular pin designs ever.

2

ABOVE AND BELOW

As with other types of jewelry, pins were made using all the popular techniques of the time. 1. A very simply carved heart. This was originally white, but has darkened through oxidation. 2. Classic, angular pins, influenced by the Art Deco movement. 3. A wonderful range of clear, reverse-carved, and painted pins.

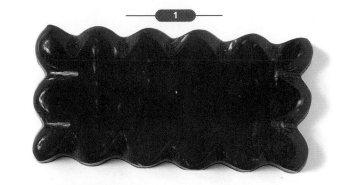

BELOW

Bar pins came in all manner of
shape and sizes. Originally the
designs were simple. 1. Bar pins
made from flat stock, plain bows
and light-carved sprays. 2. Various
European bar pins with chrome or
brass trimmings. 3. A very simple
butterscotch bar pin with little
scoring.

2

3

ABOVE

As they developed, bar pins took on more complex designs. 1. A group with light to medium carving. 2. Light to medium-carved clear and tortoiseshell bar pins, made from the side of a tube and not from flat stock.

lavish carvings as well as some of the Machine Age shapes we find in its older sibling, the bracelet.

As in most families, the parents gave this second child a little more freedom or, as we say today, a bit more "space" in which to develop. We can now see that this frivolous child took advantage. She bled the fantasies from her parental carvers, to the extent that if the Bakelite craze had lasted into the fifties and sixties it would have proved interesting to see what they would have come up with to impress the fashion-conscious consumer of those decades.

In America and Europe there was a flurry of animals being produced. Every animal you can think of has been immortalized in Bakelite. For

LEFT

Heavy-carved flowers feature on this bright red pin.

RIGHT

More interesting designs were developed. 1. Very ornate shapes. 2. Brightly-colored clear and translucent laminates. 3. This oval pin has been studded with brass stars. 4. As seen earlier, these carved bar pins were originally white, and have darkened through oxidation. 5. Manufacturers took to using more than one color, as with these bows and spray bar pins.

some reason, in the latter eighties and early nineties, there has been a revival for some of these animals. The fact that so many of them have been carved in Bakelite has made this medium a great source of coveting your favorite animal in lush reds, vibrant greens, or even in translucent ambers. Why have your favorite animal in his natural but boring color when he can be orange, green, or resin washed, or any color that takes your fancy? I have even had pink elephants.

The one animal that sits on the top of my sales charts would have to be the Scottie. Fashioned after President Roosevelt's pet, Fala, the Scottie pins are worked in all the different colors, from simple to detailed, serious to totally whimsical. These Scotties were manufactured all over the globe.

When the Machine Age vein branched out from the Deco era it took the European market in that direction, while the American craftsmen were left to the "fun and games" portion of the industry.

From Europe came the serious angular style that was associated with this avenue of Art Deco. The French were pushing out tremendous pieces, wearing the vibrant colors with trimmings of chrome, or some accented with equally colorful, but contrasting, crystal stones.

The Germans, meanwhile, trimmed some of their pieces in brass. They also took a liking to laminating translucent and opaque colors with clear colors. Some of the most stylistically great pieces attributed to the Germans are the tool pieces, which have a number of tools with Bakelite handles dangling from a Bakelite bar pin. The tools actually work: I used an auger drill approximately one inch long to make a hole in a rack base and even the bit could be removed from the chuck.

BELOW

Bow pins. 1. These stylish bows were produced using the tracery method. 2. A range of clear bows showing simple to intricate carving. 3. Very often, the same design was used on several different colors.

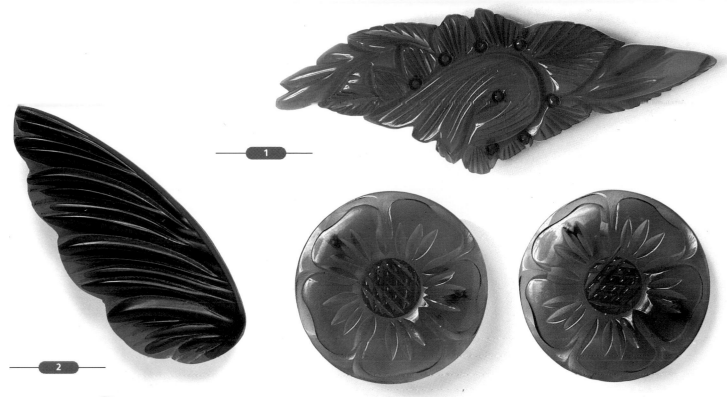

Various spray pins. 1. Clear Bakelite pins with a vaseline finish. 2. Simple, laminated sprays.

BAR PINS

The bar pin was the first of the brooches to be created. First somewhat plain, they were later carved and eventually took on the shape of ribbons and even bows.

FRUITS AND VEGETABLES

As the designers started to bore with the everyday carving of bar pins, they ventured along with their carvers into creating the fantasy pieces we find today. You as a collector can spend months in search of pieces to complete a cherry set, one of plums, or even tomatoes. I have at one time or another found all of the pieces to make up a set that consisted of necklace, earrings, pin, and bracelet. The major problem as a dealer is that, once you find the pin, it sells too quickly to acquire the other components to complete the parure. At the time of writing I did have a complete cherry set, but sold the pin which broke up the set again.

Mass production meant that many pins of the same design could be produced. 1. Very simple "hoops" in a range of different colors. 2. The same carved design on different colored rounds. 3. Various carved hoops from tube stock.

1

2

3

RIGHT AND BELOW

Round pins with figures. 1. Orange and black laminated base with "Speak no evil, see no evil, hear no evil" monkeys. 2. White and black laminated base with celluloid cameo. 3. Red and green laminated base with celluloid cameo. The last two examples were influenced by the Victorian revival.

Oval pins. 1. An orange oval with
green laminated flower as center.
2. Heavy-carved flower pin, cut from
the side of a tube and with a hollow
underside. 3. A large resin-washed
flower pin. 4. Carved and cut-
through oval with a brass base.
5. Clear red oval with reverse
carving.

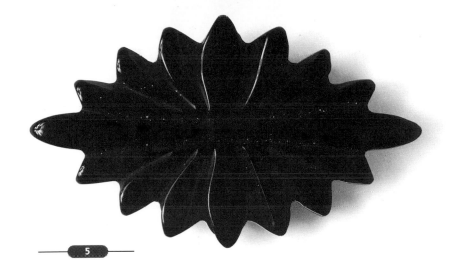

Two stylish pins in the shape of a hat. The style is a reminder of the Deco era.

A hat shaped pin based on a
European theme.

LEFT AND BELOW

1. Simple geometric sphere pin.
2. Heavy geometric pin.

1

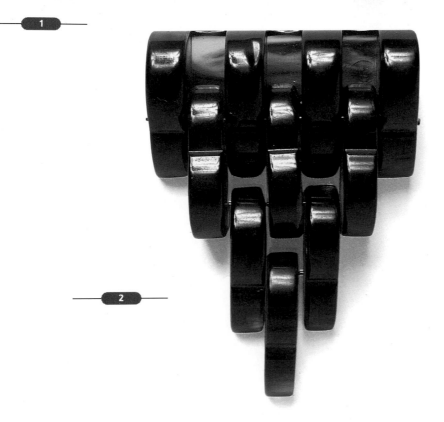

2

ABOVE AND LEFT

Floral pins. 1. Butterscotch and paint pin. 2. Laminated and layered carved flower. 3. Clear, reverse-carved and painted flower. 4. Large flower medallion pin.

A great array of pins on a floral theme. 1. Various (originally white) roses. These have often been mistaken for ivory. 2. White flower spray and two floral pins with heavy carving. 3. Rose pin of European origin with brass filigree frame. 4. Tortoiseshell colored floral pin. 5. Cobalt colored floral pin with brass trimmings, possibly of German origin.

ANIMALS

Animals formed a huge proportion of the Bakelite pins which were produced. Some were in their natural state while others took on personalities. You could wear your favorite wildlife animal or a whimsical family pet. Perhaps a horse's head or a carousel pony. I have had every animal from an anteater to a zebra, both as a normal characterization as well as dressed up in clothing with a set of great goggly eyes.

RIGHT AND OPPOSITE

Horses. 1. and 2. are resin washed. 3. A butterscotch-colored head. 4. Three pins based on carousel ponies. 5. Two zebra heads. 6. A French assembly kit of a Shetland pony with crystals highlighting features like the eyes, tail and saddle.

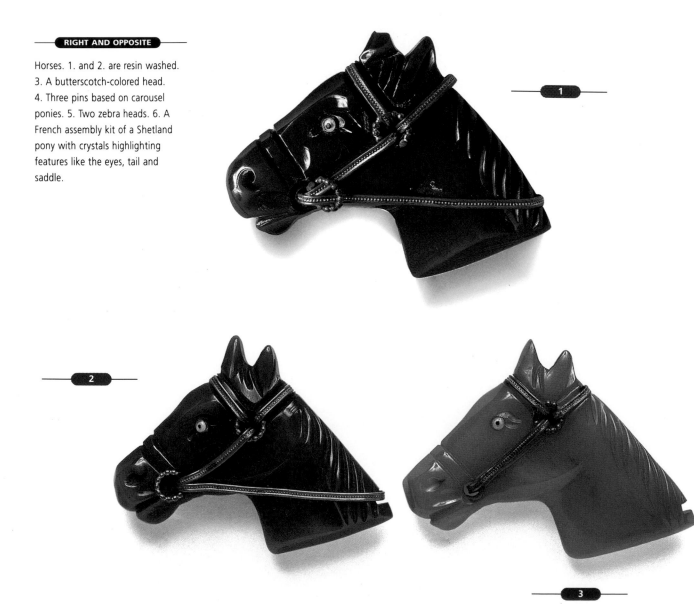

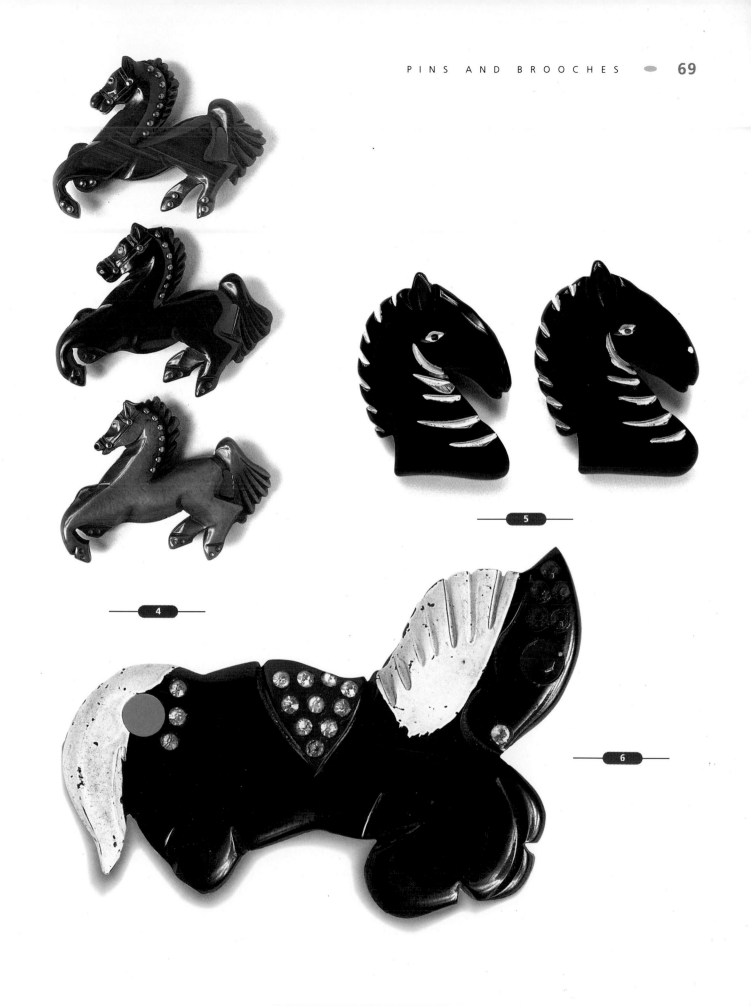

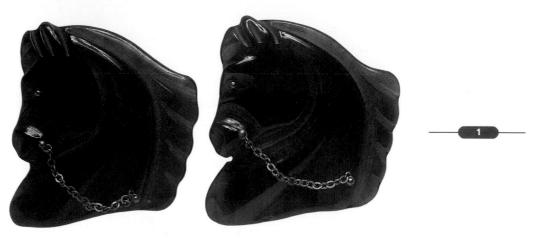

1

RIGHT AND OPPOSITE

1. Matching tortoise-colored horse
heads. 2. Various horse and tack
pins. 3. Horse pin with matching
earrings. This set is of European
design. 4. Majestic resin-washed
stallion with brass trimmings. 5. A
simple white horse pin, darkened
through oxidation.

2

4

3

5

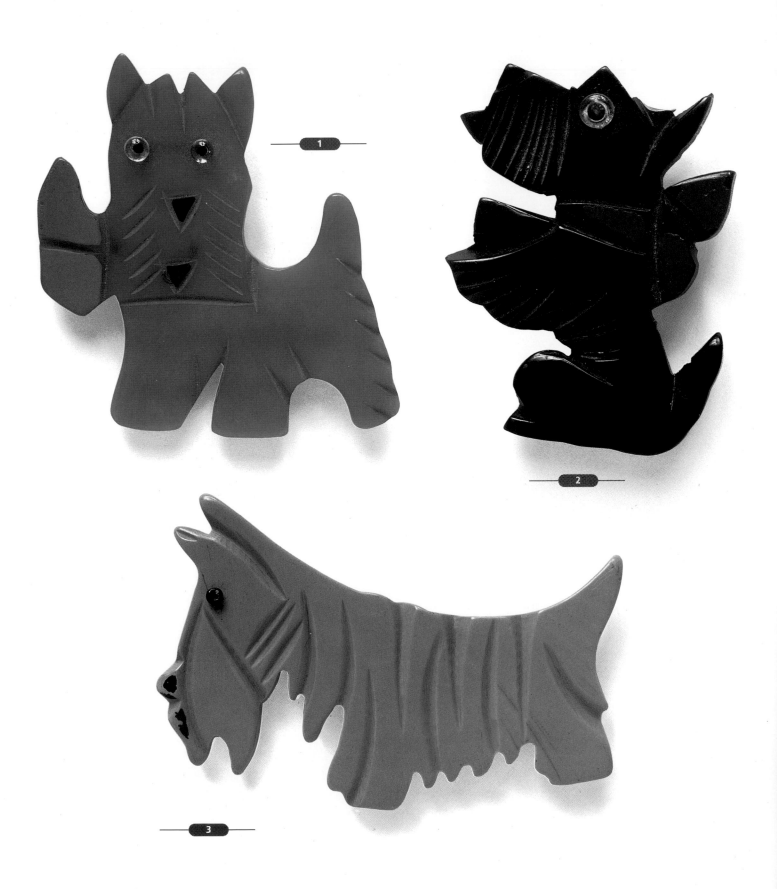

The ubiquitous Scottie dog.
1. Whimsical Scottie with a painted bow. 2. Begging Scottie, again with a painted bow. 3. White walking Scottie. 4. Flighty red Scottie on a chrome base, of French origin.
5. Small triple Scottie pin. 6. Stylized Scotties on leashes (one is a cat), of German origin.

1

Cats. 1. Pin in the shape of a cat
with a brass body and Bakelite legs.
2. Wacky cat with Bakelite head,
acrylic body, and goggle eyes.

2

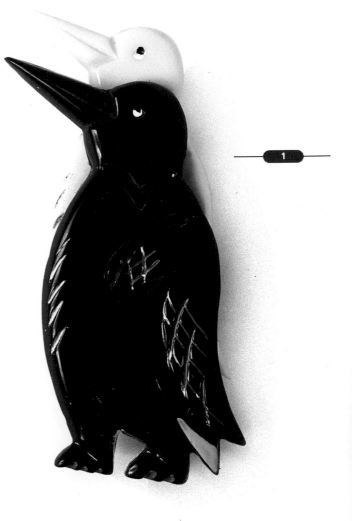

1

Birds. 1. A pair of penguins. The black one is Bakelite while the white one is made of urea. 2. Bakelite and acrylic "bird of paradise". 3. Exotic bird of European origin. The base is chrome-plated metal, while the bird's body is clear Bakelite. 4. Red bird, made in France, with paint and crystals.

Birds. 1. A selection of bird pins
laminated on wood. 2. White
rooster with painted highlights.
3. Bakelite bird with acrylic wing.
4. Two bird pins.

Insects. 1. An assortment of simple butterflies. 2. A collection of bugs from Europe! Bakelite bodies with brass trimmings.

Various elephant pins, even a pink painted one.

Two dragon pins. The black one has been cut from a tube.

Sea creatures. 1. Clear lobster pin.
2. Tortoise-colored turtle.
3. Mermaid. 4. Lobster with red
Bakelite body and acrylic claws.
5. Tortoise-colored fish. 6. Turtle
with brass top hat of European
origin. 7. Frog with brass trimmings,
also European.

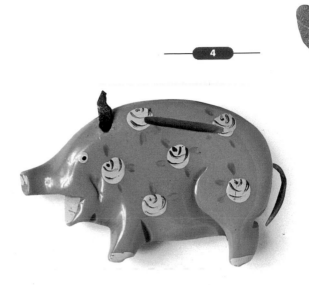

4

5

LEFT AND OPPOSITE

Other animals included anything and everything possible. 1. A black bat over a butterscotch base, originally an assembly kit. 2. Horse's head as the center of a medal pin. 3. and 4. A group of simple shapes with painted highlights. 5. White animal on an acrylic base.

MISCELLANEOUS

Everything that my mind could possibly conceive has been expressed in Bakelite pin form. The list is much too long to even start so I will take shelter under an old phrase: "A picture is worth a thousand words." The "pictures," however, represent just a small portion of what is still in dresser drawers and boxes that remain in attics, their owners still unaware of what they possess.

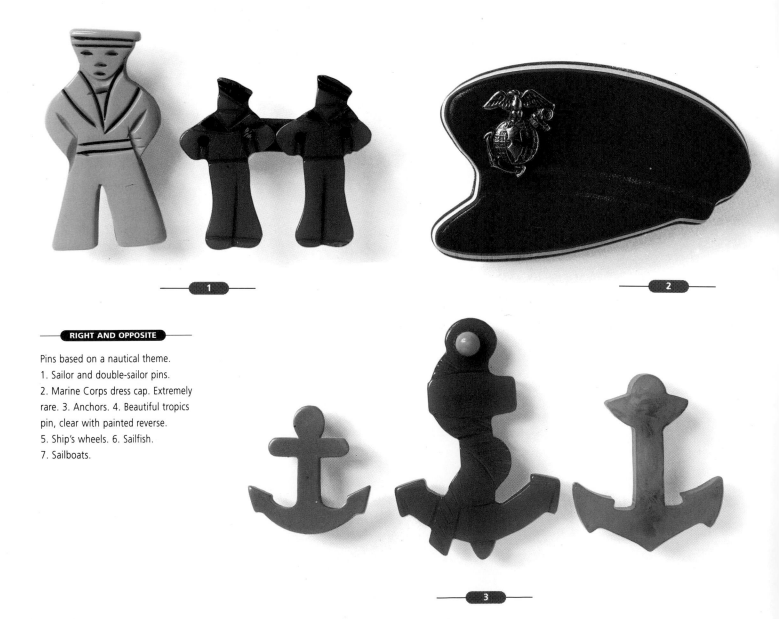

RIGHT AND OPPOSITE

Pins based on a nautical theme.
1. Sailor and double-sailor pins.
2. Marine Corps dress cap. Extremely rare. 3. Anchors. 4. Beautiful tropics pin, clear with painted reverse.
5. Ship's wheels. 6. Sailfish.
7. Sailboats.

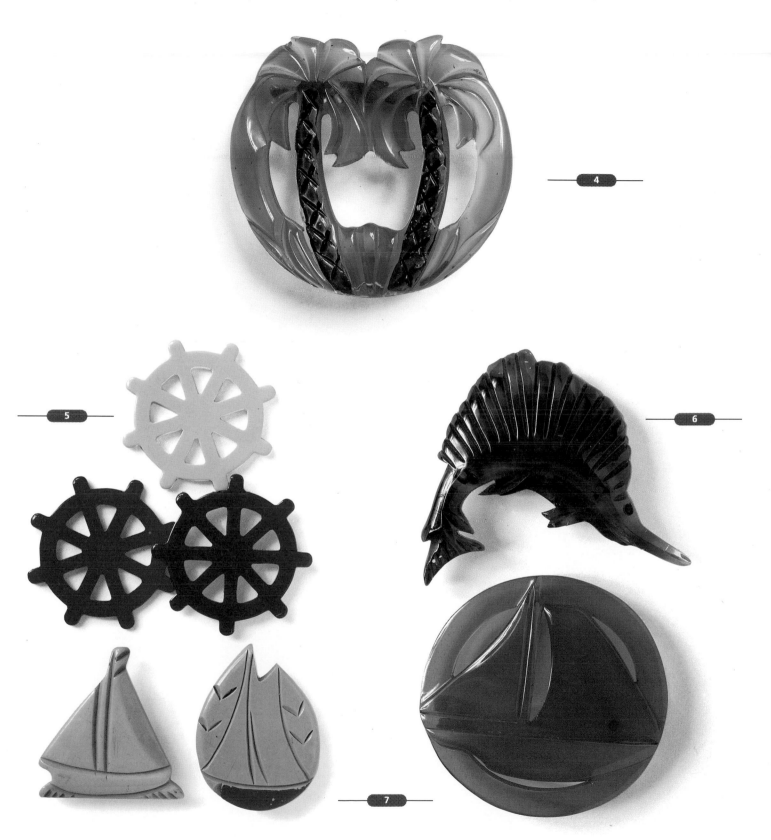

Fruit pins. 1. Extremely rare white
cherry pin. 2. Very rare strawberry
pin. 3. Classic cherry pin. The bar
and cherries are phenolic while the
leaves and chain are celluloid.

1

2

3

Heart pins. 1. 1942 cover of *Life* magazine. The model is wearing a "key to my heart" pin. 2. Heart pin with cherries. 3. Two heart pins, one with cupid's arrow.

RIGHT

An assembly kit pin from France, with crystals on a clear Bakelite round.

LEFT

Two-tone bar pin, laminated with a tracery-type carving.

RIGHT

Very rare red "Mother" pin with brass for reinforcement.

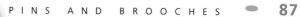

RIGHT

Crib toys.

ABOVE

Josephine Baker pin. Born in St. Louis, she lived and sang in France. She tended to have gifts made for friends. The hat is clear Bakelite.

ABOVE

Clear Bakelite watch pin.

NECKWEAR

akelite necklaces range from simple to attractively bizarre. I think that pendants were probably the first neck pieces, with beading following close behind. The pendants usually are hung from either metal or celluloid. As with the other categories of jewelry the metal signifies the European contribution, while the Americans found celluloid chain less expensive and easier to assemble.

You will find many more beaded pieces than the more extensively carved or geometric designs. The beads were cut from cast cylinders and rounded according to the shape of the designer's needs. Some were rounded and others were oval-shaped. Whatever carving they had in mind was done at this point. There are examples of faceting, as well as floral carvings. When finished with the carving, they were then tumbled

LEFT

A neckplate piece hung on a chain.

LEFT

Victorian revival pendant. Celluloid cameo on black Bakelite mount with clear Bakelite backing. This hangs on a celluloid chain.

ABOVE

Plain round beads strung on chain.

RIGHT

Carved white roses with black round beads.

ABOVE

Elongated beads, simulating amber.

ABOVE

Geometric design with multicolored half-disks.

LEFT

Very long flapper type clear necklace, simulates amber.

to a finely polished finish. The drilling was the last thing to be done. This was done in a machine which had a drill on each side and the holes were drilled to each other. The holes vary according to whatever material would be used to link them together. They used mainly cotton thread but unfortunately this material rotted over the years and many pieces have had to be restrung. I purchased a warehouse find a couple of years ago and in a box was a large number of necklaces. Each piece was individually wrapped and the cotton string was so rotted that I don't think I could separate any of the beads without the string breaking and remaining inside the beads. I restrung them all and some still had the string in the holes when I sold them.

Some of the European productions were strung on chain or were affixed to metal findings. American neckwear seemed to be fashioned to keep away the blues. More boisterous than other designers, Americans had visions of fun stuff. The fruit and veggie style carried over into neckwear completing sets that had started with bracelets. There are, of course, exceptions to every rule but this seems to be the norm. Two such exceptions are the geometric necklaces that were produced in the States and the fun tool necklaces that came from Germany.

Both continents touched on Victorian revival, and the Americans embraced the fluid and then the mechanical styles of the Deco era.

Simulated tortoiseshell necklace on a
celluloid chain.

ABOVE

Jagged rustic necklace of geometric
design.

BELOW

Cherry necklace with matching pin.
Chains are celluloid and cherries are
carved Bakelite.

A great necklace of carved white leaves over brass findings. This necklace is probably of European origin.

Cherry necklace on a brass chain.

Necklace, earrings, and bracelet with metal findings. All are part of a set of Bakelite eggs, possibly of European origin.

RINGS

FOR THE FINGERS

Anyone who can actually find Bakelite finger rings that fit is very fortunate. Those who originally wore this decorative item were certainly smaller than today's women. There are quite a few rings that do fit but they seem to be the less ornate ones.

Rings were made in the customary design of the rest of the jewelry but seem to have wandered off in number. Over the years, when Grandmother used her costume jewelry to occupy the time of her granddaughters, the rings were lost — perhaps because of their size. I have observed that most dealers may have a load of other jewelry, but just a ring or two. I seem to locate rings from the other dealers who specialize in other types of antiques.

I think the reason I have a much larger ring inventory than most is that I personally collect prison pieces, which for some reason seem to be more abundant in ring form than in the other kinds of jewelry. The prison ring is in itself an oddity. These rings were fabricated in different prisons in the United States, although I recently found a piece in Europe that seems to have belonged to a POW (prisoner of war) or perhaps an ex-soldier who was incarcerated somewhere. The bulk of these rings that I have seen, or acquired, have men's pictures in them, and seem to have a very small band. I have located a few that are larger: one with a baby's picture, and another with a picture of a woman, probably made by an

RIGHT

A multitude of plain rings.

inmate for his own wearing. Another was a man with a dog; this was also in a man's size, but I think most were made for a wife, girlfriend, or other loved one as a remembrance of the individual who was in prison.

The prison pieces were fabricated from all sorts of things. Bakelite being the most accessible plastic of the era, the creative inmate could salvage the end of his toothbrush or the bottom of his shaving brush as materials he could use. A slice off a Bakelite fountain pen made a great band on which to build the ring. I found a ring that was inscribed "N.C.S.P. '39," so I called the North Carolina State Penitentiary and was told that there were inmates who participated in recreation periods and used this time to make jewelry. Adhesives were less accessible than a match and a piece of celluloid, so the ring maker utilized the celluloid because it was flammable and he could use this to bond the pieces of the more intricate laminated pieces.

We do find rings conforming to the geometric style, both in stripes and polka dots. There are also angular-type pieces as well as the traditional floral motif. Whatever the design it is nice to find a larger ring so I can add it to my collection or fill the request of a client who needs it to complete that set she has been working on for a year or so.

The same designs and techniques were used for rings as for other pieces of jewelry. 1. Asymmetrical shapes. 2. Polka dots. 3. Carvings of flowers. 4. Stripes. 5. Fun varied shapes.

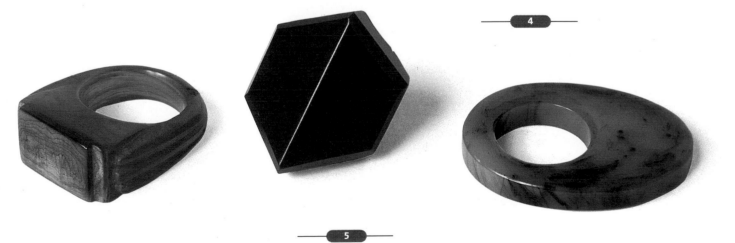

RIGHT

Bakelite ring sizer.

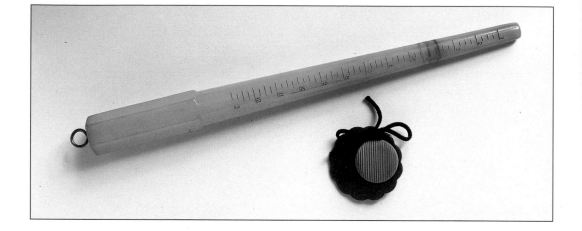

RIGHT AND BELOW

1. It is not unusual to find prison rings like this, where photographs of loved ones and pets have been incorporated into the jewelry using scraps of Bakelite. 2. This ring actually consists of up to 25 pieces of Bakelite laminated together. 3. A ring of particular interest where white celluloid has been used.

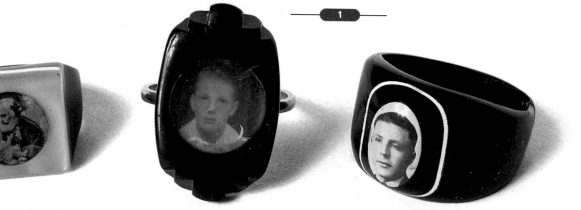

1

2

3

FOR THE EAR

Bakelite earrings are a much easier subject. They are much more plentiful and can be worn by themselves or to complement a necklace that has been fashioned out of the same thought. They come with all kinds of different findings, clips, screw backs and the less common pierced backs. Some of the earrings lend themselves to signatures, so it is more common to find signed earrings than, say, a bangle.

The earrings follow suit as to design. You can locate the floral patterns we have discussed and wear them until you find the other pieces you want, or you can enjoy them for what they are. The earring can be a funky piece in itself. You could wear huge earrings in a floral design or a pair with several beads strung down almost shoulder-length. Some were simply balls cut in half, so we can find a small pair to wear in the same color as a sweater or blouse to continue that color scheme to the ear.

They were generally part of a parure, so they are also done with the usual geometrics; if you look ahead to the collecting chapter you will find earrings taking their place among the other pieces to form complete sets.

BELOW

Clip-on and screw-back earrings were more prominent than pierced ones.

1

RIGHT

Earrings were often the final addition to a jewelry set, complementing the necklace, bangles, and pin. Therefore they are most often found to have the same designs as those popular at the time. 1. Two pairs of dangling earrings. 2. A pair of heavy-carved leaf clip-ons. 3. Long, white clip-ons.

2

3

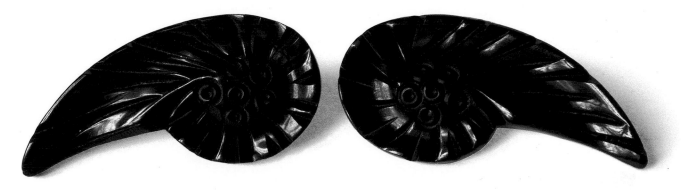

RIGHT

They ranged from anything including small shapes, either square or round, to dangling beads and pierced hoops. 1. Clip-on dangling hoops. 2. Clear carved shapes, one of Deco design, the other floral. 3. Very large heavy-carved, cobalt-colored pierced earrings.

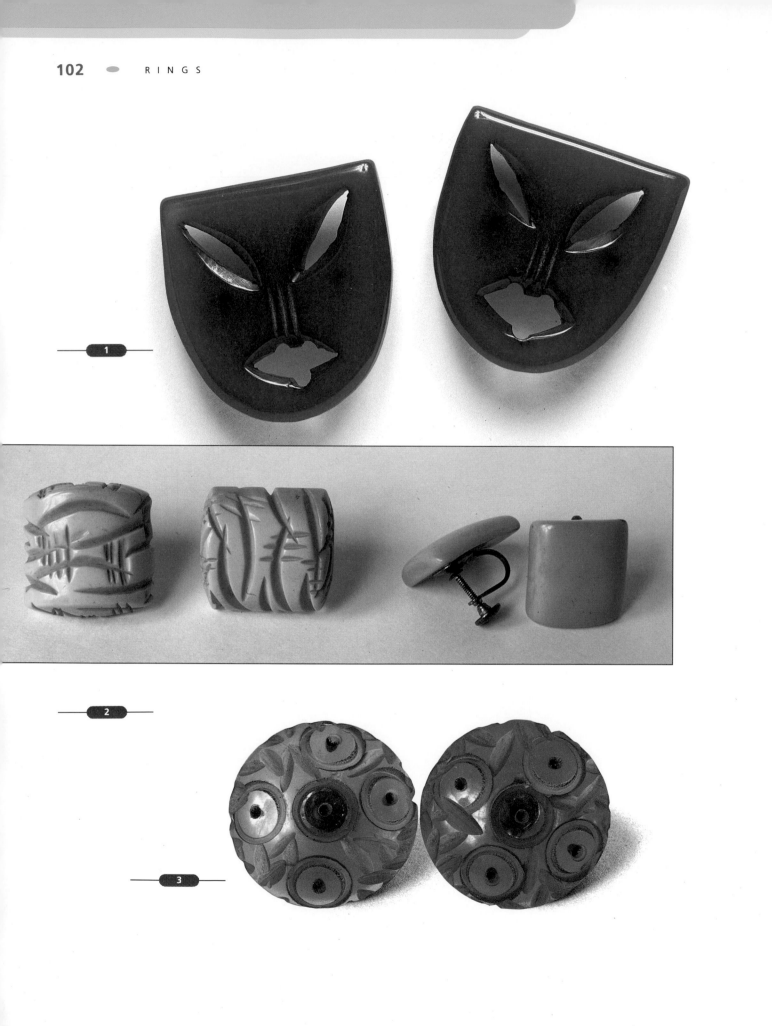

4

OPPOSITE, ABOVE AND RIGHT

1. A pair of oriental faces. 2. Two
pairs of white squares; one carved,
one plain. 3. Small, round, clear and
carved earrings, pierced. 4. Various
pierced hoops. 5. Striped screw-back
earrings, with carving.

5

here are also several cousins to the Bakelite jewelry family. In an
effort to introduce these pieces I would like to say that as a
dealer I don't have a lot of these different pieces but admire
them nonetheless. Some of the nicest carved pieces I have seen
have been clips and buckles, and there are certainly some wild pieces
that fall into this great category. I use up most of my shopping time
seeking the different types of jewelry I have outlined previously, but
when something catches my eye, I don't discard it because of its nature,
but will buy it for its beauty with the hopes of saving it or finding
somebody who appreciates the same stylish design.

The belt buckle and dress clip have a tendency to blend in with the
other pieces of jewelry. These pieces simulate some of the designs of

1. A pea-pod buckle with two carved buckles. 2. Belt buckle with matching pin. 3. White carved ornaments for use as hat pins or sewn into a blouse. 4. "End of the day" umbrella handle. 5. Cuff-links with a necktie clip, originally mistaken for amber.

bangles or pins, and I understand that the designers coordinated huge sets to tempt the consumer. I would love eventually to collect a set or 10-piece parure that consisted of earrings, necklace, pin, dress clips, bracelet, ring, and buckle. I know they existed but have yet to see all the pieces together in one place. If you look closely at some of the patterns that were carved, or the shapes that were put together, you can perceive what I mean, but is it possible now to match up all the pieces, in the same pattern, and same color, after years of separation? I have come close with some sets, as you will see in the next chapter, but I never get the proverbial cigar.

1

2

LEFT AND ABOVE

1. Handbag with clear Bakelite frame. 2. Magnificent geometric dress clips.

1. White carved belt buckles.
2. Coco Chanel-type dress clips.
3. A fantastic belt made of Bakelite links.

SECTION TWO

COLLECTING

COLLECTING BAKELITE JEWELRY

HOW DO I TELL BAKELITE?

This was the question I asked a friend years ago, and he told me to "rub it, and smell it, for an old musty smell." When I did, I got a little keener smell than he had mentioned. It was kind of a soapy, resin smell, or perhaps a burning wire insulation smell. I found out quite a while later that what I had smelled was the phenol odor associated with Bakelite. I have been told by several dealers that you can smell the formaldehyde, but having smelled formaldehyde, I rigorously disagree. What my friend and I were smelling was the carbolic acid used to make Bakelite; otherwise you would have the same odor in urea-formaldehyde products, which is totally different.

Since my own initiation, I have shown a full array of Bakelite jewelry in over 500 antiques shows. Unbelievably, I still get the "How do I tell

BELOW

Carved bracelet with acorn and oak leaf theme.

ABOVE

An example of one way to collect:
1. Same design different colors.
2. Same design same colors.
3. Same design different color and width.

Bakelite?" question, 10 to 20 times per show. My usual response is, "Use your senses — smell, sound, and touch." I always give the person a quick demonstration of what I mean. When we are finished, I usually look into the widened eyes of a newly educated and very enthusiastic Bakelite admirer, and often a new customer. I feel that if they spent the money to go to a show, then they should receive a little courtesy. Unfortunately, like any business, there are a few dealers that have told me that "educating them is a waste of time" and I actually heard a New York dealer at a Pier Show tell a woman, "I don't have the time to waste on someone who isn't going to buy something." If a dealer will not help in your education then move immediately to one who will. Granted, this woman was not going to buy a $500 pin, but after I spent five minutes explaining how Bakelite was developed, she did spend $150 on sets of mah-jongg jewelry for her partners in Ohio, where she was returning, to enjoy her Sunday night game with the girls. My main point here is that some dealers have let Bakelite go to their head and no longer partake of the joy and camaraderie that can be experienced by collecting Bakelite. I think you will find that most Bakelite dealers are a fun-loving and extremely friendly lot.

STARTING YOUR COLLECTION

I would strongly suggest the first step in collecting Bakelite is to find a dealer who

1) has a large inventory of at least 100 pieces of Bakelite (if they have other plastics also, this is an extra feather in their cap),

2) has a fair knowledge of the different plastics, and

3) will take the time to help you in your quest for knowledge.

Spend some time with this person. Have them show you how to get the phenol smell. I have handed bracelets to people and asked them to rub and smell, and when they barely touch and sniff (which produces nothing at all), I do the rubbing for them and let them smell my thumb, which always gets a sort of bewildered reaction. So rub that bracelet hard and fast as though you wanted to raise a blister; then, when your thumb becomes very hot, smell quickly because the odor will dissipate in about two seconds.

When you have accomplished this, the next move is to buy a group of several bangles or other pieces. Explain to the dealer you want to do some experimenting at home. Vary your selection according to the types of plastic: some Bakelite, celluloid and acrylics (lucite), and spend as little as you can ($10 or less per piece). Label the bracelets or pins as to their composition so that you will be able to decipher which is which at a later time.

When you get your purchases home you can set up your area for experimenting. If space is tight, go to a hardware store or lumber yard and purchase a sheet of plywood about 2 feet x 2 feet, or 2 feet x 4 feet this will provide you with a mobile work area. Next you will want a couple of small boxes in which to store the bracelets and the following tools:

1) a toothbrush (very stiff),

2) pliers (flat jaw, not serrated or tongs),

3) a small sharp knife,

4) a hacksaw blade (fine-toothed), and

5) assorted grit sandpaper (200, 400, 600).

You can add to your tools as you go along, but these will do for now. You may also want to set up your work space near the hot water faucet or a stove to boil water.

As a preface to our next operation I would like to mention that I have overheard dealers and buyers alike telling a novice Bakelite collector

ABOVE

White hinged bracelet and pin. Both are inset with a black Bakelite oval and celluloid cameo.

that the best way to tell Bakelite is "to stick a hot pin in it." Never have I heard them explain what is supposed to happen. Several things can happen, and unfortunately one of them is that if you stick a red-hot pin into a very old piece of celluloid, it may fly out of your hand and remove your eye. If you recall, nitrate is used in explosives, and older celluloid is cellulose nitrate. You could also ruin a very nice piece of celluloid or acrylic. Besides, it will be difficult to convince a dealer to let you stick a hot pin into a piece before you buy it. Incidentally, if it is Bakelite nothing will happen, but not everyone is aware of this. You may see a small purple dot if you use a magnifier. This is the color Bakelite burns: no matter what color the piece is, it will always leave a purple or burgundy type of mark. I would much rather see people use the following techniques.

SMELL

Take your Bakelite piece and run it under your hottest faucet water, for about 30 seconds, and smell quickly. This should release the phenol smell. If not, then dip your piece into boiling water and smell it again. If the piece is really Bakelite or another phenolic, you will get an odor.

The next step in our experiment is to take the pieces that you have labeled celluloid and acrylic, and dip these. At extremely hot

ABOVE

Four-piece set in translucent burgundy and brass trim, of German origin.

Various reverse-carved and painted bracelets.

temperatures you may pick up a slight camphor smell from the celluloid, and a smell somewhat similar to automobile oil from the acrylic. If the water is not very hot, you will not register any odor. I want to stress this phenol odor as much as possible, because once you get the smell you will never forget it. This can be your rule of thumb at shows, when you are buying pieces for your collection. If it has the familiar phenol odor you can never go wrong.

Recently I had a beautifully carved red bangle which seemed to be a bit off-color. Most of the people who came to my booth would pick it up, look at it, and, somewhat puzzled, return it to the rack and buy other pieces that made them more comfortable. A dealer eventually asked if it was actually Bakelite. I responded that initially I had my doubts, but after smelling it was convinced and, thinking it was a great piece, I bought it. He rubbed it himself, and jokingly asked a woman beside him if she wanted a "hit." She indulged in getting her whiff of phenol for the day, and they happily left with this great red bracelet, which they had proved was indeed Bakelite. The piece in question had been the product of oxidation, and had turned the strange color probably as a result of contact with perfume or some other chemical.

Horse pin with pin glued onto back. Note the mold hole. This is not Bakelite but a molded celluloid piece.

Buttons and buckle with the same design.

FEEL

Once the items have cooled, you may also want to try the thumb rubbing on each piece. This should be done after the articles have been in the hot water, so that you can melt all the layers of wax and polish off each piece, especially because people have said Bakelite is a slippery substance. In fact, once stripped of its polish and wax coatings, Bakelite actually has an abrasive feel. You should notice that your thumb will heat up rather quickly with the Bakelite, and that the other plastics will feel more slippery to the touch. Again, you can also smell the phenolic resin smell from the Bakelite, whereas you will never attain a smell from the cooled thermoplastics.

Take the different pieces, and drop them together into a container of hot water for about three to five minutes. Being careful not to scald yourself, retrieve them with pliers or tongs, and as soon as they are cool enough to handle but still hot, try to bend, twist, and knead them. You will notice that the thermoplastics have become pliable and the thermoset phenolics are still rigid.

SOUND

Another experiment that can be performed is to hold a Bakelite piece lightly between your thumb and forefinger and gently tap it, if possible, with another piece of Bakelite. The resulting sound is similar to the tapping of two pieces of bamboo; a dull, hollow, thud type of sound. I have found that I can get the sound I'm looking for by simply flicking a piece with my fingernail. When the same thing is done with other plastics, the sound is more of a higher-pitched, clacking sound. This method will also come in handy when you are more experienced. When you have a bangle that you know is Bakelite but the sound is not quite there, I have found that, on closer inspection, the bangle will have a crack or it will have been repaired. The cast bangles seem to have a tempered-like quality, and when cracked or repaired, never regain that bamboo sound. Remember this, as it will save you from buying pieces that you may discover later have been damaged or repaired.

IS IT OLD OR NEWLY MADE?

There is a particular reason for carefully wording the above question. I could have said, "Is it old or new Bakelite?" This is similar to asking, "Is it old or new amber?"

Amber, in order to evolve into its present form, has let nature take the sap from a tree, and compress and petrify this sap for thousands of years, or more. In my mind how do you classify anything that old as new? Granted, they do grind up and emulsify cuttings and sweepings from the work area, selling this as reprocessed amber, but it is still amber.

Bakelite is similar. All of the Bakelite jewelry that you see today is old Bakelite. It was cast from the mid-twenties up until the early forties when the formula was sold to Union Carbide. I think Union Carbide bought the formula primarily to make way for the cheaper and less sturdy plastics which they were trying to market at the time. The Marblette company produced until the early fifties. There isn't any company producing cast phenolic jewelry today, because of the cost. They would first have to acquire the resins. The extreme heat and pressure process used to cast the phenolics is too costly. The machines, jigs, and vacuum systems (the fine dust produced in carving has to be collected so that it is not ingested) used to carve the pieces, as well as the tumblers to polish them, have mostly gone to the boneyard. I don't think you can find a

ABOVE

Tower of European work, mostly French.

business manager today who would recommend that his company retool and incur the kind of expense it would take to indulge a whim that is restricted to the antiques and collectibles field.

I have heard so many stories on the show circuit that there is new Bakelite in circulation, and in 10 years of collecting and dealing I have yet to hold a piece in my hand. There are a few dealers who claim every piece you show them is "new Bakelite" but of course they would buy it for a pittance to help you out, if you'd let them, and you could return to see it a week later, at a very hefty price. There are too many ways for the knowledgeable enthusiast to tell. I have seen acrylics that boasted to be Bakelite. I even went to an auction in New York, with my father-in-law, that promised, "hundreds of tubes, rods, sheets, as well as finished pieces of 'Bakelite'." When I arrived, the owner first admitted to having

ABOVE

Translucent burgundy set with the same carving on earrings, bracelet, and pin.

Marblette, but ultimately came clean (after 15 minutes) and agreed that most of what he had was in fact styrene and acrylic. The only Bakelite I saw during the entire sale was a piece or two his wife purchased, to use as patterns, for their "new Bakelite."

The long and the short of it is that the bulk of what is called "new Bakelite" is in fact another polymer. The difference can be detected in many ways. The presence of the color white is an immediate indicator. There is no longer a white-colored Bakelite.

I have just envisioned collectors and dealers falling to the floor with this statement, but I prove it to people at shows every week.

Quite a while back I picked up what I think was a salesman's sample kit (it may have been a promotional board for a store counter). My first glance made me ask if perhaps the individual who made up this kit was indeed color-blind. The disks had the corresponding colors printed beneath them, but in no way did they coincide with the sample itself. When I had the time, I sat down and sanded the tops of all the disks. I couldn't believe the transformation: back to the colors that were specified in print. Each disk now revealed the color that was labeled below it.

If you take a Bakelite mah-jongg cube (generally a light yellow to a mustard color) and cut it slightly with your hacksaw blade, you will find a brilliant, white stripe where you did your cutting.

Most of the books I have read on Bakelite state that Bakelite colors faded. Having played and experimented many times with different pieces, I am prepared to argue the point that Bakelite did not fade, but in fact darkened with age.

The white mah-jongg cube turned to a much darker mustard color. Put a cut or chipped mah-jongg piece on a sun-exposed windowsill for a month or two, and see if the altered area doesn't change, so that you barely notice where the cut was. If you take a piece of Bakelite jewelry, and find an inconspicuous area to sand with your 200 grit paper I guarantee that you will be amazed. You will find that mustard will turn to white. Some of the weird, dark green colors will lighten to a rich cobalt. Some of the lighter oranges will shine a pastel pink. Dark greens turn a light jade color and the best one I have found is a light greenish orange that reveals a light blue. These are colors that some of the most adamant collectors have yet to behold. If you finish the sanded area with 600 grit paper and leave it on your windowsill, in 30 days you will be hard pressed to figure out where you sanded.

Bangles and napkin rings demonstrate this color change process. If you look inside, then outside you will find the inner areas much lighter than the exposed outer area. The same is true with the fronts and backs of other pieces.

Over time you will find quite a few examples of what I refer to as newly manufactured items from old pieces of Bakelite. There are people who comb the old findings warehouses throughout the country, in search of old Bakelite parts. These are generally found at flea markets, dangling on modern chains. There are some buttons that are made into earrings. There are all kinds of pieces that are utilized and sold as finished products. The best way to tell these is to look at the findings or

ABOVE

Pin and buckle from the same carver.

Tortoiseshell-colored stripe on celluloid chain with matching pin.

fastenings used. Most of these pieces, you will find, have findings (which were purchased at the local craft shop) hot-glued or superglued onto an old piece of Bakelite. Neither of these adhesives existed at the time when the Bakelite was produced. What you want to see, if you are looking for original construction, is a pin-back that is two separate components, set into holes drilled into the plastic. Another method used is two tabs on the back of the pin-back, which were pressed into holes that were drilled at back angles, and the tabs have been pressed back into the angle of the holes. The third method was a bar pin that has rivets or screws, fastening the pin to the body. Giveaways for necklaces are the chains that were used. The greatest amount of neckware used the celluloid chains of the twenties and thirties, with some of the American and many German designers utilizing solid brass chain. Some of the French designers used chromium-plated brass and copper for chains as well as accent parts. If the chains or pin-backs do not fall into one of these categories, then you should take a much closer look. You will also see jewelry that was made from gaming pieces — for example, mah-jongg and domino bracelets, with pins and earrings that match. The bulk of the dealers know what is original, and can tell you the story behind each piece. I personally keep any of these pieces I get separated in a designated case.

Tower of identically carved but different colored bangles.

These pieces are by Ron and Esther Shultz. They are classified as "newly made" Bakelite, and have all been created from original Bakelite.

RON AND ESTHER SHULTZ

About eight or nine years ago, while on a shopping spree at the huge flea market in Brimfield, Massachusetts, I stumbled upon a husband-and-wife team, who had dedicated their life to reworking and making Bakelite jewelry from salvaged pieces of Bakelite. I still remember the awestruck feeling that came over me then; the same feeling returns each time I see their display.

Ron and Esther Shultz, who come from Pennsylvania, make it difficult for one to decide which of the two is more talented. The Shultzs buy any old pieces of Bakelite they can find. It may be a cracked radio cabinet or a broken piece of jewelry, but Ron or Esther can transform this discarded item into a piece of art. They not only copy some of the well-known pieces, but have also used their imaginations to inspire other designs.

They are both very closed-mouthed as to the methods that are used, so there is little that I can say about how the pieces are done. I will say, though, that it is hard to tell with an untrained eye that each is a piece that was recently created. They do have signs all over their booth explaining that their work is "new work from old pieces," and the copies are made to a slightly different scale, so as not to confuse them with the original. Through this method of advertising it is hard to imagine that they are trying to deceive anyone, or corner the repro market. Their work was done for several years without signature. They started signing their pieces with a paper label around 1993, but found that the label was being removed, so now they use a carving device to engrave the name

Stretch bracelet and similar style pin with black Bakelite laminated over white Bakelite.

deep into each piece. Each piece is a labor of love; they fully disclose that the work is new; their prices are very reasonable (I feel their prices are actually too low for some of the artistry involved). I have even sent people to them to purchase particular pieces that are not available on the open market. I gather that there is actually a sort of cult taking form, with people building collections that consist of strictly Shultz pieces. I recently identified a couple of early Shultz pieces from the collection of one of my better customers. She asked if I could take these pieces to them when I saw them again, and have them sign them for her.

The pieces that went unsigned are easily spotted by the exaggerated luster in the finish. Again I have never been told how they do it, but, if forced to speculate on the process, I would say each piece was sanded to almost a 1600 grit finish and polished with a jeweler's rouge to accomplish the glass-like texture. Bakelite was tumble-polished in the thirties and this method never achieved the overpolishing found on a Shultz creation.

Two identical white bracelets with oriental theme and stones inlaid.

WHERE TO FIND IT

I feel the best place to start your Bakelite collection would be at an antiques show. The main reason is that, while you are still a novice, you want to deal with people who know what they have, and can prove to you that what they are selling is what they are representing it to be. These dealers are also in the business for the long haul, and you will be able to find them at a later date. They are constantly looking to generate new business. For example, when you graduate into "bigger and better" things, they will often take some of your earlier, less elaborate, or more common pieces in trade for that mega-piece you have been lusting after for several weeks. I have had several pieces regenerated four or five times. It gives me stock for my newer collectors, and it also helps the older collector to cull out their collection, so that they will wear most of their pieces on a regular basis.

You will pay a little more at antique shows, because the dealer incurs a much higher overhead, but you will benefit in the long run. You can make a dependable friend in the dealer who helps you through the infancy of your collection. This dealer will keep in contact with you and call when he picks up that killer piece that you asked them to look for.

RIGHT

Various clear colored bangles. Bangles like these do bring a premium if clear.

You will find that your collection will always consist of Bakelite that you can wear or trade. I have had too many people come to ask me to show them how to detect a piece of Bakelite, then immediately go it alone, because they wanted to "save money." When they enthusiastically show me their "super finds," I can't bring myself to explain that "Yes, $30 would have been a great price for that bracelet, if it were Bakelite, but what you bought was a $7 piece of lucite."

After you have been collecting for a while and you feel more confident, then it is time you forage through the flea markets, church sales, and junk shops, rubbing elbows with those obsessed with finding the ultimate treasure for short money. In these places, you will generally find mediocre pieces at reasonable prices. Sometimes you will stumble across a piece that is labeled lucite, celluloid, or even wood, that is actually a great Bakelite discovery.

Dealers in other fields will often knowingly come across Bakelite in a house lot they purchased, but will sell it very cheaply because they didn't pay as much as a Bakelite dealer would have to. When dealing in primarily Bakelite, you have to pay more for things in order to keep a large and varied inventory. Incidentally, a good point to mention at this point is that you should also keep an eye out for any Bakelite that is very cheap, no matter what it is, because these pieces can often be sold to a beginner or used for barter.

Cherry pin with hearts and cherry
necklace set.

HOW MUCH SHOULD I PAY?

Because of the large number of variables, I would say the best answer to
this question is to pay what you are comfortable with. If a piece you find
is rare, in pristine condition, in a more desirable color, it is likely that you
will spend top dollar. If it is in poor condition or, more importantly,
damaged, then the price should be drastically reduced. Over the years I
have had people bring pieces to be repaired and, after they added up
their initial cost and the repair bill, they have a great piece at an
extremely reduced cost. It is fine if this works out; it is hard to view a
collection of chipped and broken Bakelite with pride when it has cost a
fortune and you will never recover what you put into it. Newly or custom-
made Bakelite should always be purchased at a reduction in comparison
to original pieces. If you find that a dealer is trying to get top dollar, then
he is in the business solely for the money, and I would suggest that you
contact someone like the Shultzs, as their merchandise can be had at a
more reasonable price, and will eventually accrue in value.

I would recommend that somehow you create a system to keep track of the price trend in your area. This way you can establish a guide for yourself, as you cannot spend all your time double-checking prices of magnificent pieces of Bakelite. When I put killer pieces out for sale, the "to die for" piece usually leaves my booth within a few minutes of the show opening. The first people see it, but run off to check the price with other dealers, then come back to find it has been sold.

Four-piece set with brass findings. Tortoiseshell-colored Bakelite with brass sea horses.

HOW TO COLLECT IT

The mental process, probably the most interesting part of collecting, is as varied as the collectors themselves. Viewing the patterns of my own family members, I have witnessed many transformations. My wife Alexandra started with multicolored laminated pins and hinged bracelets, until I acquired a magnificently clear, "carved to death" piece. Then we sought out clear pieces, which stopped her heart. After amassing several clear pieces, she came across a pattern in a bangle that she liked. After finding several identical bangles, varying only in color, the picking

Four bangles, same carving but
different color and width.

Prison set made from black Bakelite
bonded with white celluloid and
topped with the mercury cameo
from a mercury dime.

slowed, and then she picked up on sea-type figurals. The hunt is exciting and constantly changing.

Angela, at a mere fifteen months, will spend hours playing with crib pieces. Her only prerequisite is bright multicolored pieces. She seems to enjoy the noise her clunky pieces make. My daughter Alex is simply content with maiden bracelets, necklaces, and pins, as long as they are fashioned in her favorite color, green. The collectors mostly indulge in a whimsical manner. Some collect figurals, others a particular style or color; many are into fruits and vegetables. There are also the parure collectors, who are constantly on the prowl for that pin that will match the necklace, bracelet, earrings, and dress clips, all with the same carvings and same color that took them the last six months to garner. The beauty of collecting Bakelite is that there are no boundaries, and once you have put together one collection you can shift into another assortment, without missing so much as one breath.

HOW TO CARE FOR IT

Now that you are swept up with that Bakelite fever, you will need things to do at night, when the shows and the shops have closed. I find that a great method to relax, and plan my quest for the following day, is polishing Bakelite. Whenever I find a piece for my own collection, I whip

RIGHT

Three wide bangles, all with the same diagonal pattern.

out the old toothbrush, and give that piece a nice hot soapy bath. Clean all the road dirt and layers of whatever off, then give it a nice towel-drying. Now apply a healthy amount of polish and scrub away.

Simi-Chrome seems to be most commonly used but Top Bright will do just as well. Both come from Germany and smell, feel, and work the same. I have found that if you go to an auto-body supply, you can pick up a gallon of rubbing or polishing compound for the same price as a small tube of the others. I have a buffing wheel that I use with the rubbing compound first (to take out small scratches), then the polishing compound. If you do polish by hand, work the toothbrush and mixture of your choice rigorously into all the nooks and crannies. Remove all excess polish, by scrubbing under very cold water. The last step in our manicure is with an old towel; buff out your piece until you achieve a uniform rich luster. Your pieces should be stored away from direct sunlight and, when transported, should be wrapped up in soft paper, or cloth, and not allowed to rub or bang against each other, for the result will be dull abrasion marks, or even chips, if hit too hard.

I would like to thank all of you again for buying my book and for your friendship and support. I sincerely hope, that I have been able to help you enter into what I feel is a most exciting and enjoyable pastime. Good luck in your quest and may an affordable "Philadelphia Set" cross your path.

INDEX